© SHUTTERSTOCK

Among the great women of the Bible—Eve, Sarah, Hannah, Mary the mother of Jesus, Phoebe, Lydia, and Priscilla to name a few—stand Ruth and Esther. While each of these women bear witness to God's grace on behalf of His people, only Ruth's and Esther's stories have been recorded as Bible books. Sometimes overtly and sometimes subtly, in each of their lives we see God act in love for the sake of His mission of seeking and saving the lost through His Son, Jesus Christ. The books of Ruth and Esther are not only for women, however. All people of faith—women, men, and children—will see in these books themselves, their situations, and above all, their Savior, Jesus Christ.

ENRICHMENT MAGAZIN

IN THIS ISSUE ...

TO THE DIRECTOR

This student folder contains nine study leaflets and the enrichment magazine. Remove the center staple and distribute the leaflets as indicated in the leaders guide. This magazine should be distributed at the first session for use throughout the course.

3558 S. Jefferson Ave., St. Louis, MO 63118-3968
1-800-325-3040 • cph.org

Written by Gary L. Dunker

Edited by Robert C. Baker

Cover illustration by John Cox © Concordia Publishing House

Graphic design by Karen Pauls

This publication may be available in Braille, in large print, or on cassette tape for the visually impaired. Please allow 8 to 12 weeks for delivery. Write to Lutheran Braille Workers, P.O. Box 5000, Yucaipa, CA 92399; call toll-free 1-800-925-6092; or visit the website: LBWinc.org.

Manufactured in the USA.

4 5 6 7 8 9 10 11 12 13   33 32 31 30 29 28 27 26 25 24

The mission: land Allied forces on the beaches of occupied northern France!

For Such a Time as This

To help plan the mission, an accomplished military leader was chosen, someone who made impossible missions possible. The leader was General Dwight D. Eisenhower. "Ike" to his friends, Eisenhower was a graduate of West Point Military Academy and had served under Generals Pershing and MacArthur. In 1944, and at fifty-four years of age, he headed the Supreme Headquarters Allied Expeditionary Forces. Indeed, with his background and bearing, Dwight D. Eisenhower was "born for a time such as this."

God gives you and me missions that at times may seem impossible. However, God makes no mistakes. When He assigns a mission, He also provides the way to complete it. As examples, we can look to the missions of Esther and our Savior, Jesus Christ. By God's gracious will, their impossible missions became possible. Esther and Jesus were given their missions "for such a time as this" (Esther 4:14). But so were you!

© SHUTTERSTOCK

Esther's Mission—Free Her People

A queen has privileges: servants, chefs, and the finest of everything. Plus protection, power, and prestige! However, Queen Esther's husband, the powerful Persian king Ahasuerus, had one law that even she dared not break:

> If any man or woman goes to the king inside the inner court without being called, there is but one law—to be put to death, except the one to whom the king holds out the golden scepter so that he may live. (Esther 4:11)

This law would strike fear in any heart. Perhaps Esther had never seen this law enforced. No one dared break it!

Esther stood outside the inner court . . . waiting nervously. Perhaps she wondered, "How did I, a lowly Jewess, come into the presence of the King of Persia? How did one such as I become his queen?" The answer plays again—she became queen when the former queen refused the king's law "to show the peoples and the princes her beauty" (Esther 1:11). Then the king gave "her royal position to another who is better than she" (1:19).

Esther was poised and beautiful. Mordecai, her relative and a fellow Jew already in the king's service, took care of her until one day she pleased the king. Ahasuerus loved Esther more than any other woman, so he set his royal crown on her head and made her queen instead of Vashti (Esther 2:17).

Recalling the murderous plot Mordecai discovered, Esther knew that she should follow Mordecai's advice and tell Ahasuerus of Haman's plan to kill their fellow Jews. "And who knows," Mordecai said, "whether you have not come to the kingdom for such a time as this?" (Esther 4:14).

Esther may have thought that God's mission for her was impossible. So she prepared for her mission by fasting for three days. She sought the Lord's counsel. Following the fast, Esther stood outside the inner court . . . waiting. In her reply to Mordecai's advice, Esther responded, "I will go to the king, though it is against the law, and if I perish, I perish" (Esther 4:16).

"What is it, Queen Esther? What is your request?" the king asked (Esther 5:3). Words spring forth like water from a fountain. Salvation awaits Esther's people. God placed Esther where He wanted her "for a time such as this."

Jesus' Mission—Free Us from Our Sins

Jesus' mission? It was to accomplish our salvation by shedding His blood on the cross (Hebrews 9:14) and by rising again for our justification (Romans 4:25). This would be an impossible task for a mere human being, but Jesus was and is the Son of God (1 John 4:15), the very Word of God made flesh (John 1:14).

Following His Baptism, Jesus endured and then overcame the devil's temptations and refuted him with God's Word (Matthew 4:1–11). Sin was great, but God's love for humankind was greater: "For God so loved the world, that He gave His only Son, that whoever believes in Him should not perish but have eternal life" (John 3:16).

In His final days, Jesus set His eyes squarely on Jerusalem, His city of opposition, knowing that humiliation and death awaited Him there. While in the garden, He prayed three times for God to remove the cup of death from His lips.

Nevertheless, as our substitute, He faithfully submitted to His Father's will: "Not what I will, but what You will" (Mark 14:36). John the Baptist had proclaimed, "Behold, the Lamb of God, who takes away the sin of the world!" (John 1:29). On the cross, the world's sins, your sins, were taken away by Jesus—forever. The cross and the vacant tomb stand witness to the freedom from sin that Christ won for you and for all people.

Jesus' Mission—Free Us from the Law That Condemns

Jesus' mission was not limited to offering His life passively to satisfy God's wrath because of our human rebellion. Jesus' mission was also to satisfy God's demand for a life of perfection and holiness—an active living out of God's will in His life.

Far too many Christians overlook or even are ignorant about this aspect of Jesus' mission. They assume that while Jesus died for their sins, it is up to them to please God through living a life of perfect holiness on earth in order to have a genuine relationship with God. Jesus did His part, they believe, and now they must do theirs.

But the Scriptures clearly refute this claim (see Romans 7:20–25; 1 John 1:8–9). Not only did Christ come to die for our sins, which we in our sinful state could not do for ourselves, Christ also came to obey God's Law perfectly for us. He freed us from our sins *and* He freed us from the Law's condemnation.

What joy you and I have knowing that "when the fullness of time had come, God sent forth His Son, born of woman, born under the law, to redeem those who were under the law" (Galatians 4:4–5a). Then Paul adds, "So that we might receive adoption as sons" (Galatians 4:5b).

In Baptism, you became God's son or daughter. God applied to you not only Jesus' sacrificial death but also Jesus' perfect life. In Baptism, you were joined with Christ in His death and resurrection (Romans 6:1–4). Now God sees you as perfect, holy, and righteous in His sight, all for the sake of Christ. Set free from sin, you are enabled to live your life in righteousness and holiness (6:18, 22).

Your Mission

God has given you a mission too. In fact, He has given or will give you several missions throughout your life. Sometimes our missions may seem impossible—being a faithful husband, a loving mother, a helpful neighbor, or a loyal employee. Just as he tempted our Lord in the wilderness, the devil tempts us to abandon our missions. And if Satan isn't successful in getting us to abandon them, he'll tempt us to treat our family members, neighbors, and employers with disrespect, disloyalty, and disdain.

But it needn't be that way. Like He gave to Esther and our Savior, God not only gives us our missions at just the right time, He also provides us with the courage to accomplish them by His grace. God may not call you to storm an embattled beach, but He will strengthen you for your many tasks. Even now, He is working in you "both to will and to work for His good pleasure" (Philippians 2:13). Your mission is God's mission, and He is "able to do far more abundantly than all that we ask or think . . . to Him be glory in the church and in Christ Jesus throughout all generations, forever and ever. Amen" (Ephesians 3:20–21).

Sandaled Feet

Runners make a foolish mistake when they buy shoes on looks alone. Shoes are a runner's most important piece of equipment. Consequently, wise runners spend hours checking out shoe after shoe for just the right fit.

In the Bible, we read primarily about only one type of shoe—a sandal. There were options though. Sandals could be crafted out of leather, wood, or reeds. However, in spite of their simplicity and limited styles, there were important times in salvation history when sandals were on the scene. Let's take a look at some sandals in the Bible and the feet that wore them.

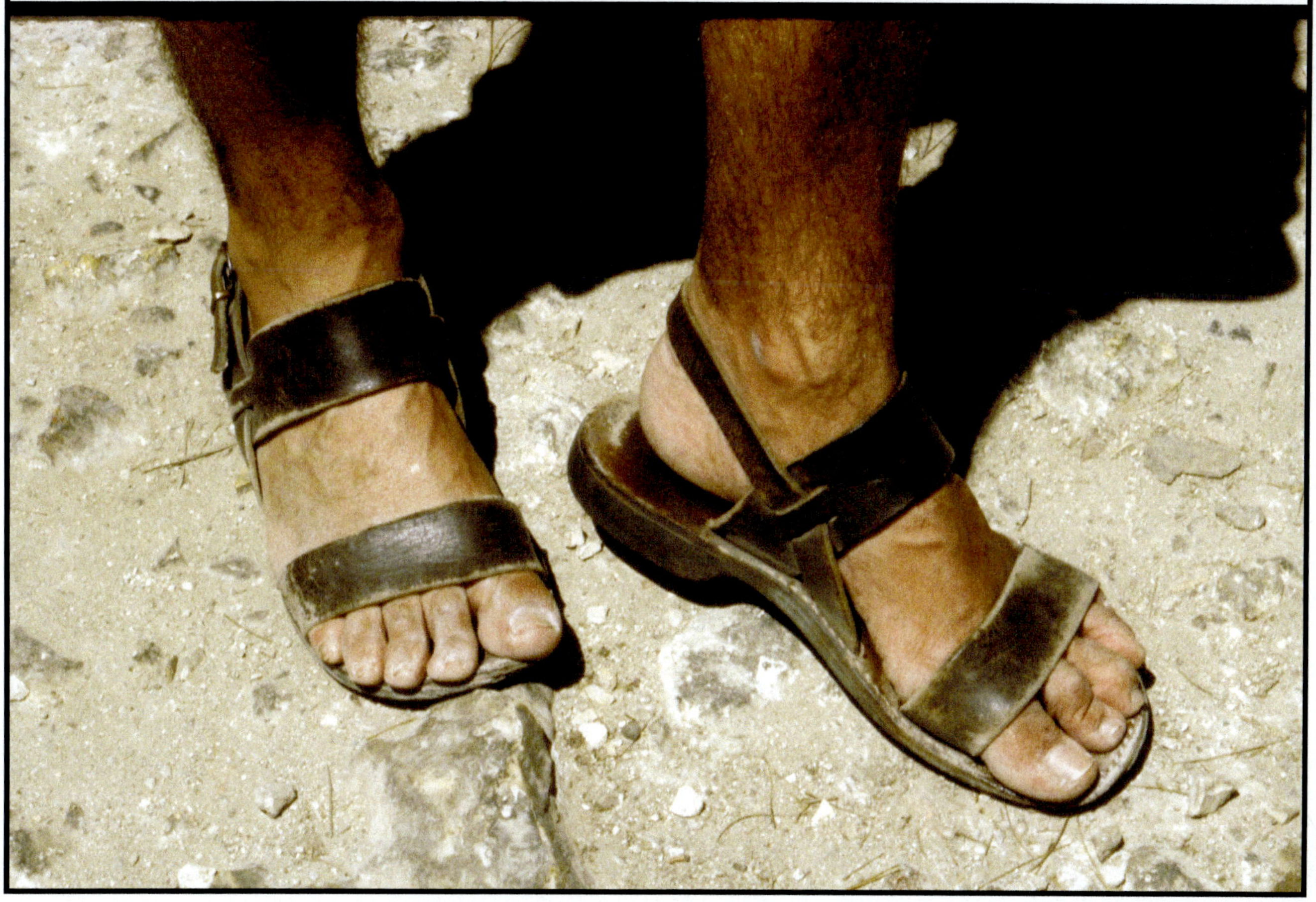

Moses

While tending his father-in-law's flock, Moses saw a burning bush and was drawn to it. From within the bush God called out, "Do not come near; *take your sandals off your feet*, for the place on which you are standing is holy ground" (Exodus 3:5; emphasis added). This special manifestation of God's presence is called a *theophany* (thee OFF uh nee). In the Bible, theophanies were those rare occasions when God was present in a special way or appeared to human beings to commission them or to deliver a special message.

In Moses' day, the first thing someone entering a holy place did was remove his or her sandals. God required this of Moses. Only after Moses recognized his inability to approach God apart from His grace was his heart prepared to receive the commission God had in store for him (Exodus 3:10). God would strengthen Moses for the task set before him: to play a role in the salvation of His people.

Boaz

When you study the Book of Ruth, you will come across a story of how Boaz got a sandal handed to him. In Boaz's day, giving someone a sandal meant the end of a transaction—real estate or otherwise. When Naomi's next of kin, her kinsman-redeemer, took off a sandal and handed it to Boaz, he took away any obstacles preventing Boaz from redeeming Naomi's land (Ruth 4:8) and marrying Ruth. That is exactly what Boaz did—with someone else's sandal!

Joshua

Like Moses, Joshua was once told to take off his sandals. Right before the battle of Jericho, Joshua met a man with a drawn sword (see Joshua 5:13–6:5). The man introduced Himself as commander of the Lord's army. He gave Joshua a command like the one God gave Moses: "*Take off your sandals from your feet*, for the place where you are standing is holy" (v. 15; emphasis added).

Like the area surrounding the burning bush, the ground surrounding this heavenly commander was holy because God had manifested His special presence there. The second-century theologian Origen (185–254 AD) believed that the man Joshua met that day was the pre-incarnate Christ. Origin wrote, "Who else is the prince of the host of the virtues of the Lord, save our Lord Jesus Christ?" The defeat of Jericho would belong to God, not Joshua.

The Israelites

After the return of the spies from Canaan, the Israelites revolted against Moses. Eight spies said, "No, we cannot conquer Canaan." Two said, "Yes, we can—with God's help." The Israelites sided with the eight spies. Because of Israel's unbelief, God kept them in the desert for forty years (Numbers 14:20–24, 33–34). While the older, unfaithful generation died away, the younger generation grew to maturity. At last, God's time was right to allow His people to cross the Jordan River and to begin conquering Canaan.

Moses told the Israelites, "I have led you forty years in the wilderness. Your clothes have not worn out on you, and *your sandals have not worn off your feet*" (Deuteronomy 29:5; emphasis added). In spite of their disobedience, God sustained them—even down to their sandals. Through forty years of desert wandering, God preserved His people and kept His promise to bring them to the Promised Land. If God kept His promise to them, He will certainly keep all His promises to us!

John the Baptist

Matthew records an incident involving John the Baptist and sandals—not John's sandals, but Jesus' sandals. John commanded the Pharisees and Sadducees to prove their repentance by leading God-pleasing lives (Matthew 3:8). Yet John also preached to them about the coming Messiah. "I baptize you with water for repentance," John told them, "but He who is coming after me is mightier than I, *whose sandals I am not worthy to carry*" (Matthew 3:11; emphasis added).

In John's day, untying, removing, or carrying the sandals of one's master was considered a job for only the lowliest of servants. John knew that Jesus was God's promised Lamb and, in faith-filled humility and repentance, he willingly submitted to his Master, Jesus Christ. Although John was a great prophet, Jesus was even greater because through His sufferings and death He would become the "least in the kingdom of heaven" (see Matthew 11:7–12).

Your Spiritual Sandals

In Ephesians 6:10–19, Paul reminds us of the spiritual armor that God has given us to protect us from head to toe. God's armor wards off Satan's fiery arrows of temptation, despair, and disillusionment. Like a well-fitted Roman soldier whose feet also are prepared for battle, God has given us spiritual shoes, "sandals" if you will. We are made ready to run because of the Gospel of peace that we have through Christ, our Lord (v. 15). Our spiritual sandals, made ours through the blood of the Lamb, enable us to march quickly against a ferocious enemy as we wield the "sword of the Spirit" (v. 17), the Word of the living God.

Sandals in the Bible

Runners know that the correct shoes prevent injury and enhance performance. However, how many times do we fail to put on the sandals ("shoes") of readiness as God commands us through Paul to do? Trusting in our own abilities and presumed spiritual power, we look to ourselves instead of to our gracious, giving God. In such instances, we are not ready to "run with endurance the race that is set before us" (Hebrews 12:1).

However, thank God that He and He alone provides us with His rich forgiveness through Christ, our Lord. Through His Word of Law and Gospel, He prepares us for running our race in this life and to achieve the crown of eternal life. That crown has already been won for us by our Savior. Enjoying God's peace through His Son, we join Paul in pressing "on toward the goal for the prize of the upward call of God in Christ Jesus" (Philippians 3:14).

Jesus' Disciples

In his Gospel, Mark tells us about another pair of sandals—not Jesus', but those of His disciples. When Jesus sent His disciples on a Galilean preaching tour (Mark 6:7–13), He commanded them to "travel light." "He charged them to take nothing for their journey except a staff—no bread, no bag, no money in their belts—*but to wear sandals* and not put on two tunics" (Mark 6:8–9; emphasis added). Taking only their staffs and their sandals, they would be enabled by God to produce signs and wonders to confirm their powerful message.

What about you? You may worry that you do not have enough. But Jesus says, "Do not be anxious about your life, what you will eat or what you will drink, nor about your body, what you will put on. . . . your heavenly Father knows that you need them all. But seek first the kingdom of God and His righteousness, and all these things will be added to you" (Matthew 6:25, 32–33).

The Language of the Medes and Persians

If someone put this symbol,  before you, would you know what it means? Perhaps you see two interconnected triangles that look like the Star of David, a symbol of the Jewish faith and the modern state of Israel. Look again! In the world of alchemy, this symbol represents *arsenic,* a word with Persian origins.

It is possible Esther learned, heard, and spoke an ancient form of the Persian language in the court of King Ahasuerus. At one time, the Persian Empire stretched from the Mediterranean Sea as far east as the Indus River in India and as far south as Egypt. Early Persians recorded their words in cuneiform, a wedge-shaped writing form etched into wet clay that was allowed to dry. About the second century BC, an alphabet appeared among the Persians. This alphabet remained in existence until around the seventh century AD when Persia became part of the Muslim world.

Over the centuries, many traditional Persian words have become part of our Anglo-Saxon (or English) lexicon. When other nations began to trade for Persian wares, the natural progression was for the language to migrate also—or at least some of its words. It may surprise you to learn that you already know some Persian words. Look at the following chart to see how many you recognize. In the left column are the English words. In the middle column, find a definition of the word, and on the right, find the original Persian word.

Ancient peoples often carved important documents such as contracts, shipping lists, and maps on stone or clay tablets. This map of the world (ca. 700–500 BC) from ancient Babylonia (modern Iraq) contains a cuneiform inscription and a map of Mesopotamia. The ancient capital of Babylon is located in the center of the map, and the concentric circular area represents an area called the "Salt Sea."

PERSIAN WORD LIST

Anglo-Saxon Word	Definition	Persian Original
Arsenic	Highly poisonous compound	Zarnikh
Azure	Sky blue color	Lajaward
Bazaar	Oriental market	Vachar
Beige	Grayish yellow color	Bysses
Bronze	A metal of copper/tin	Berenji
Caftan	Ankle-length coat-like garment	Qaftan
Candy	Crystallized sugar	Qandi
Carafe	Bottle with flaring lip	Qarabah
Caviar	Eggs of various fish served as food	Khaviar
Checkmate	The winning position in chess	Shahmaat
Cummerbund	A broad waistband	Kamarband
Cushy	Pleasant, posing little hardship	Khush
Divan	Collection of poems by the same author	Dipi vahanam
Jackal	Doglike scavenger	Shockal
Jasmine	A climbing fragrant flower	Jasman
Julep	Cool drink of syrup, sugar, and herbs	Gulab
Khaki	Light yellow-brown color	Khaaki
Kiosk	Vending stand with open window	Kushk
Lemon	Fruit with thick yellow skin	Leemo
Mogul	Person of great wealth	Mughul
Pajamas	Loose fitting trousers	Paejamah
Percale	Smooth cotton cloth with plain weave	Pargalah
Pilaf	Rice cooked in spicy liquid	Polu
Rhubarb	Plant with red or green edible sour stalks	Rivaas
Rice	Seeds of a particular grass, often cooked	Riz
Rook	Castle-shaped chess piece	Rokh
Saffron	Crocus plant cultivated for its flower, dried stigmas used for flavoring	Zafaraan
Scarlet	Brilliant red color	Saqalat
Seersucker	Light cloth with raised and flat stripes	Sheershekari
Sherbet	Cold drink of sweetened and diluted fruit juice	Sharbat
Spinach	Vegetable with wide dark green leaves	Esfanaaj
Talc	A powder applied to the skin to keep it dry	Taalc
Turban	Male head covering	Toorband

Why So Many Different Languages?

Long before Esther spoke her first word in Persian, the Bible tells us that "the whole earth had one language and the same words" (Genesis 11:1; see also vv. 2–9). However, the sin of spiritual pride overtook humankind as it sought to make its name great and to ascend the heavens by way of a magnificent tower. God's response? Destroy the tower of Babel, confuse human language, and scatter people across the globe. Our pride today merits God's anger, and we see its disastrous results: our communication becomes mere babbling, and we are separated by sin from God and from each other.

However, on Pentecost, God in His grace overturned that fateful day in Babylon. God's Holy Spirit enriched Christ's disciples with the power to speak the same message in many different languages (Acts 2:6). The Gospel—God coming down to us in Jesus Christ rather than us trying to raise ourselves to God—is the source of our reconciliation and hope. In all languages, Christians now carry the message of forgiveness and faith wherever they go: Christ died for our sins and rose from the dead to give us eternal life (Romans 5:19–21).

CHRIST,
OUR KINSMAN-REDEEMER

Perhaps you can recall a time when stores offered Green Stamps. Many years ago, when someone made a purchase at a store, a clerk would count out a number of Green Stamps that their purchase earned. Once at home, one licked the Green Stamps and pasted them into a specially designed Green Stamp book. Maybe you can recall your mother or father periodically taking out the Green Stamp book to determine what merchandise to "redeem" with

the stamps. When enough stamps were collected, the book of stamps was mailed in, and in a few weeks, the merchandise arrived.

Long before the invention of Green Stamps, God put in place a way to redeem back "merchandise"—and people! In the Book of Ruth, we read the term *redeemer* a total of five times (Ruth 2:20; 3:9, 12; 4:6, and 14). Let's look into Ruth and see how it points forward in time to Christ, our Kinsman-Redeemer. He has redeemed us not through stamps placed in a savings book but with the price of His own blood.

The Role of Kinsman-Redeemer

To learn more about the role of a kinsman-redeemer, we must travel back to the time when God gave Moses the set of laws contained in Leviticus. Here the concept of kinsman-redeemer appears for the first time (see Leviticus 25:47–55). Leviticus outlines the responsibilities given to an individual's near blood relative. A kinsman-redeemer must come to the aid of a financially poor relative. Should a financially poor relative sell himself or herself into slavery to pay off debts, the kinsman-redeemer must buy back the relative's freedom. God apportioned the land to each Israelite family as a sacred trust; guarding this trust also became the responsibility of the kinsman-redeemer. The redemption of land by the kinsman-redeemer prevented the accumulation of large portions of land at the expense of the poor. If poverty forced the sale of land, the kinsman-redeemer of the original landowner had to buy back the land, if possible.

In the ancient Jewish culture, the male head of the household held all property rights. As such, when a man had sons, those sons remained in the father's house even after they had married. Only upon his father's death did a young man inherit any property. Should a young man die leaving a childless widow behind, his brother was duty-bound to marry the widowed woman and sire children so that the dead man would have an heir for his property.

Naomi's two sons, Mahlon and Chilion, would have provided for their mother upon the death of their father. Since neither son left behind any children when they died, we may conclude that each died early in their marriages. The death of these two young men meant that Naomi and Ruth had no one to care for them. Their lives became dependent on the generosity of others. Only if a near blood relative, a kinsman-redeemer, stepped forward to fulfill his obligation to buy the land Naomi received upon her husband's death, could they hope to survive. Rental income provided some relief, but it was insufficient to support them. Whoever married Ruth also assumed responsibility for the welfare of her mother-in-law, Naomi.

Naomi and Ruth

For Naomi, the famine that struck Israel stole the comfort she once possessed (Ruth 1:19–21). It is possible that rains did not fall in Israel for a time yet fell in the hills on the opposite side of the Jordan River, leaving Moab with ample crops. When Naomi's husband and sons died in Moab, Naomi found herself dependent on the charity of others. At last, the famine that gripped Israel left, and Naomi returned home. Naomi's best hope for survival rested in the hands of her kinsman-redeemer, because her old age made it impossible for her to glean the grain left in the fields.

Naomi's life runs parallel to ours. In our lives, sin has taken away our comfort. As sons and daughters of Adam, we live in a constant state of animosity toward God. "None is righteous, no, not one," Paul writes in Romans 3:10. Original sin spreads just as one rotten apple infects the entire basket (Romans 5:12). As Naomi's best hope rested in the hands of her kinsman-redeemer, our only hope for rescue out of our sin comes from the death and resurrection of Jesus Christ (Ephesians 1:7).

Similarly, Ruth's situation seemed as hopeless as Naomi's did. Ruth left behind her family and placed her faith wholly in Naomi's God. God did not disappoint; He massaged the heart of Boaz until he agreed to redeem the land Naomi owned and to take Ruth as his bride with the understanding that Boaz would provide Mahlon with an heir (Ruth 4:9–10). Ruth, the Moabitess, becomes the ancestress of King David and Jesus Christ (Ruth 4:18–22; Matthew 1:5).

Boaz

In Boaz, we witness a nature and kindness reminiscent of our loving Lord Jesus Christ. From the first moment he met Ruth until he agreed to take her as his wife, he showered kindness and compassion upon her (Ruth 2:8, 14–16; 3:15–18). Boaz also looked with favor upon Naomi. In love, he welcomed Naomi into his household, redeeming her and obligating himself to care for her as if she were his own mother (Ruth 4:9).

Jesus, Our Redeemer

Some people mistakenly think that they can earn their own salvation. These people believe that God considers their "good deeds" as exchangeable for His heavenly kingdom—"Green Stamps," if you will. When they do some "good deed," they think that God licks another "Green Stamp" and pastes it into their book of life. However, Scripture declares, "For all have sinned and fall short of the glory of God, and are justified by His grace as a gift, through the redemption that is in Christ Jesus" (Romans 3:23–24).

God has justified us through His Son. The "Green Stamps" that redeemed us were not our good deeds but the precious and holy blood of our Lord and Savior Jesus Christ. Paul writes, "For you know the grace of our Lord Jesus Christ, that though He was rich, yet for your sake He became poor, so that you by His poverty might become rich" (2 Corinthians 8:9). The old hymn "The Church's One Foundation" (*LSB* 644) puts it this way:

The Church's one foundation
 Is Jesus Christ, her Lord;
She is His new creation
 By water and the Word.
From heav'n He came and sought her
 To be His holy bride;
With His own blood He bought her,
 And for her life He died.

English painter Thomas Matthews Rooke (1842–1942) is known for his collection of paintings entitled *The Story of Ruth* (painted 1876–77). In this selection of three in the series, Matthews portrays Ruth in separate scenes with Naomi, Boaz, and Obed, the grandfather of King David. Perhaps reflective of Rooke's unassuming style, English painter Edward Burne-Jones, who served as Rooke's master, said of him, "Also there is a very high place in heaven waiting for him and he doesn't know it."

The Feast of Purim

How do you celebrate the Fourth of July? Where I live (Lincoln, Nebraska) the city sets aside the whole day for family fun. One of the local parks hosts a celebration that ends in a spectacular fireworks display with patriotic music, timed to the fireworks, broadcast over a local radio station. Family and friends come over. I grill hot dogs and hamburgers, while my wife, Carol, lines up all the other goodies, such as baked beans, tossed salad, corn on the cob, and desserts. (Boy, do we love the desserts!) When it gets dark, we take out the lawn chairs and watch the fireworks from our backyard.

Jews celebrate the Feast of Purim with equal vigor. As you will see, on the fourteenth day of Adar (roughly our month of March). Jewish people still celebrate with great joy what God did for Esther and Mordecai. Let's look at this Jewish religious holiday and how it lends itself to learning more about Christ.

Reading the Megillah

One important Jewish tradition on Purim, the reading of the scroll of Esther, has long occurred on the fourteenth day of Adar. About the third century AD, a rabbi suggested that Jews read the Megillah (the scroll of Esther) on the eve of Purim as well, and that women hear it read. After all, the actions of a woman, Queen Esther, delivered them. If someone cannot attend the reading of the Megillah in the synagogue, it can be read at home, as long as the reader is male and over the age of thirteen.

Another tradition involves raucous hissing, stomping, and the use of a *ra'ashan*, a traditional noisemaker spun by hand, at the mention of Haman's name. This happens some fifty-four times during the reading.

The Purim Megillah (Scroll)

Hamentaschen Recipe

Hamenstachen, a Jewish Purim tradition, goes by many names. Among these names, is the Yiddish *Homentashn*, which means "Haman's pockets." In modern Hebrew, *Oznei Haman* means "Haman's ears." (Jewish people love desserts too!) Regardless of their name, you can enjoy these pastries anytime. Although Jews consider a sweet poppy seed filling traditional, feel free to substitute apple butter, prunes, cherries, or even pineapple.

- 2/3 cup butter or margarine
- 1/2 cup sugar
- 1 egg
- 1/4 cup orange juice (smooth, not pulpy)
- 1 cup white flour
- 1 cup wheat flour (*do not* substitute white flour)
- 2 tsp. baking powder

Various fillings

© IRAL TEITEBAUM / ISRAEL IMAGES.COM

Blend butter and sugar thoroughly. Add egg, and blend thoroughly. Add orange juice, and blend thoroughly. Add flour, 1/2 cup at a time, alternating wheat and white. Blend thoroughly between each addition. Add baking powder with your last half cup of flour. Refrigerate batter several hours (overnight is best). Roll batter as thin as possible between a sheet of parchment paper and a sheet of waxed paper lightly dusted with flour. Dough is sticky. Cut out 3- or 4-inch circles.

Place a small amount of filling in the middle of each circle, folding the sides to make a triangle. Fold the last side under the starting point, so that each side has a corner that folds under (this prevents the filling from falling out). Do not completely cover the filling.

Bake at 350° for 15–20 minutes, until golden brown but before the filling boils out.

Yield: Using a 4 1/4-inch cutting tool should yield about 20–24 cookies. Enjoy!

Food Gifts and Other Acts of Charity

Traditionally, Jews celebrate Purim as "days for sending gifts of food to one another and gifts to the poor" (Esther 9:22). In keeping with this tradition, everyone over the age of maturity hands out brightly decorated baskets filled with food, candy, and other snack items. These baskets go to relatives, neighbors, friends, bosses, schoolteachers, and even family doctors.

Most Jewish people donate to the poor during Purim. They gather these donations at the synagogue. Among the Jewish people, even the poorest individuals *must* donate to the poor during Purim.

The Traditional Purim Meal

Like our traditional Fourth of July meal, a traditional Purim meal accompanies this holiday. Purim calls for a more lavish meal than normal, featuring wine and meat. Traditionally, Jewish families eat their Purim meal on Purim afternoon. Should Purim fall on the Sabbath, the Purim meal should end early enough in the afternoon to enable a good appetite in time for the Sabbath meal.

It is also traditional to enjoy a special triangular fruit-filled cookie known as *Hamentaschen* (see attached recipe) while celebrating Purim. *Kreplach*, a dumpling filled with cooked meat, chicken, or liver and served in soup, may also make up part of the traditional meal.

Masquerading

Some have called the Feast of Purim the "Jewish Mardi Gras," but a better comparison is Halloween. Masquerading became part of the tradition of Purim in the fifteenth century AD when Italian Jews adopted the customs from Roman carnivals. For a time, some clerics spoke to no avail against the practice of masquerading on Purim. In many locations, including Israel, masquerading occurs on Purim as men, women, and children annually parade in costumes and masks.

The Singing of Songs

Singing and a special prayer belong to the traditions of Purim. Songs include "From the Beginning of Adar, Joy Increases," and "The Jews Had Light and Gladness, Joy and Honor"—based on Esther 8:16. Often the Jewish people will sing or recite a special prayer, known as *Shoshanat Yaakov*, at the end of the Megillah reading.

Other Traditions

The Fast of Esther on the thirteenth of Adar commemorates the fasting of Esther, Mordecai, and the Jewish people (Esther 4:16). This fast originally happened on the fifteenth, sixteenth, and seventeenth days of Nisan (during Passover), however, rabbinical tradition forbids fasting during Passover, and so the Fast of Esther now begins on the thirteenth of Adar.

Family Purims—many Jewish families celebrate "family Purims" to commemorate their escape from persecution, accidents, or other misfortunes.

A Reason for Christians to Celebrate

For the Jewish people, their deliverance from death at the hands of Haman is a cause to celebrate. Unfortunately, manmade traditions can hide the true reason for celebration. Christmas and Easter, for example, can be so overshadowed with secular and personal concerns that we fail to celebrate the significance of these occasions. Far more serious, however, are those occasions when we show contempt for God and His Word by refraining from preaching and God's Word.

As we read in Esther, God saw the plight of His people and sent a "redeemer." For the salvation of the world, Jew and Gentile alike, God sent His own Son, Jesus Christ. By the spilling of His precious blood on the cross, God delivered us from sin and death. We Christians celebrate this deliverance every Sunday when we remember Jesus' atoning death and His powerful resurrection. As contemporary Jewish people today sing songs celebrating their deliverance from evil Haman each Purim, we who believe in Jeshua the Messiah, Jesus the Christ, sing a song of our eternal deliverance in Him:

This is the feast of victory
for our God. Alleluia.
Worthy is Christ,
the Lamb who was slain,
whose blood set us free
to be people of God.
Power, riches, wisdom,
and strength,
and honor, blessing,
and glory are His.
This is the feast of victory
for our God. Alleluia.

IN LEAGUE WITH SATAN

For many people, the word *holocaust* sends chills up their spines. I remember a time when my daughter and I toured the Holocaust Museum in Washington DC. After she read a placard describing the transportation of Jewish people to their deaths, we had to take the "long way around" a boxcar that was once used for that hideous purpose. The thought of what ordinary men and women endured at the hands of others was more than my daughter could handle. She could not pass through the boxcar even if it meant missing exhibits on the other side. She was overcome with the horror of the Holocaust.

Although the word *holocaust* appears with religious connotations in the Bible (it is usually translated "whole burnt offering"), when you and I hear or read *holocaust*, we usually think of the atrocities committed against Jewish people and others during World War II. Unfortunately, the Holocaust of the 1930s and 1940s was not the only time when cruel individuals have sought to destroy the Jewish people.

The Book of Esther points to Haman as someone who wanted to destroy the Jews. Matthew's Gospel points to another: Herod the Great. You and I readily think of a modern example, Adolf Hitler. Influenced by Satan, these men and others sought to destroy the people from which God had chosen to bring forth the Savior promised long ago (see Genesis 12:3, 7; 13:15; 24:7; Galatians 3:16). In His grace, God chose the life of His Son as a guarantee of His promise to protect those whom He loves (Psalm 91:14).

Haman

To this day, Haman's name lives in infamy. Every time Purim is celebrated by modern Jewish people and the Megillah (the Book of Esther) is read, they "boo" or use noisemakers to drown out Haman's name. In the days of King Ahasuerus, Haman served as the king's vizier. The Bible tells us that Haman was the son of Hammedatha, an Agagite (Esther 3:1). This fact seems to indicate that Haman descended from Agag, king of Amelek, whom King Saul spared and Samuel killed (1 Samuel 15:8–33), making revenge a possible motive for Haman's actions.

Haman plotted to kill Mordecai and all the Jews exiled in Persia. When Mordecai discovered Haman's insidious plan, he relayed the information to Queen Esther, herself a Jewess. Haman drew lots to determine the date that all the Jews would die and built a scaffold on which to hang his enemy Mordecai (Esther 3:7; 5:9–14). The lot fell on the thirteenth day of Adar (our February–March). Esther foiled Haman's plot by revealing Haman's plan to King Ahasuerus. "Who is he, and where is he, who has dared to do this?" Ahasuerus asked. "And Esther said, 'A foe and enemy! This wicked Haman' " (Esther 7:6).

Instead of watching Mordecai hang from the gallows he had ordered built, Haman was hanged there. By God's grace, the Jews avoided extermination, a tragic holocaust. Queen Esther gave Haman's home to Mordecai, and King Ahasuerus granted Mordecai a position of high authority (Esther 8:1–2).

Herod

Called "the Great" because of his many building projects among the Jewish people, including the rebuilding of their temple, Herod (37–4 BC) also lives in infamy. Among the list of those Herod had killed are his second wife, Mariamme; her grandfather, mother, and brother; and two of his own sons, Aristobulus and Alexander. Rome granted Herod permission to kill a third son, but Herod died five days before the execution could take place.

When the Magi visited Herod, "he was troubled" (Matthew 2:3). Among his titles was "King of the Jews," so when the Magi asked, "Where is He who has been born king of the Jews?" (v. 2), the thought of a new rival galled him. With the Savior already born, Satan schemed to rid the world of its Redeemer by orchestrating the murder of Bethlehem's innocent boys in an effort to kill the Christ Child before He could grow into manhood.

Matthew records that Herod "killed all the male children in Bethlehem and *in all that region* who were two years old or under" (Matthew 2:16; emphasis added). Accounts vary on the number of children ages two years and younger who died at the hands of Herod's forces. The murder of these infants is tragic. However, it is important to remember that regardless of how much power this Herod wielded, God preserved His plan for our salvation.

While Herod committed his holocaust in and near Bethlehem, God was rescuing Jesus and His parents. Warned by an angel, the holy family had already fled to Egypt (Matthew 2:13–14). God's plan of salvation came through Christ despite Satan's attempt to thwart it.

Left: This seventeenth-century AD Hebrew miniature depicts the banquet of Ahasuerus (Xerxes) and Queen Esther, also attended by Haman.

Top: This bronze coin (ca. AD 43), now on display in the Israel Museum in Jerusalem, shows Herod Agrippa I, King of Judea.

Hitler

During his time in power, Adolf Hitler (1889–1945) oversaw the orchestrated mass murder of millions of Jewish people and others, including the mentally and physically challenged, Gypsies, political opponents, and a number of Roman Catholic and Protestant clergy. The Nazi pogrom against the Jewish people in particular has added a new and even more sinister depth to the word *holocaust*. In addition to its religious meaning of a whole burnt offering to God, in our secular language today, *holocaust* also refers to Hitler's deliberate persecution and murder of the Jewish people.

In 1935, the Nuremburg Laws reclassified Jews from German citizens to German subjects. Intermarriage bans followed, as did shops displaying "No Jews Allowed!" signs. When German Jews protested, violence erupted throughout Germany. Jewish synagogues and stores were burned in a Nazi response. Adolf Hitler personally authorized the extermination of the Jews in 1941. Death camps sprang up with the sole purpose of killing men, women, and children. Even non-Jews can recite the names—Buchenwald, Dachau, Auschwitz, Majdanek, Treblinka, and Sobibor. The word *Holocaust* now recalls the over eleven million lives ended by Adolf Hitler.

During the Nazi period, German workers and schoolchildren would have been familiar with this official 1938 poster of Adolph Hitler that reads, "One people, one empire, one leader."

A Christian Response

Sin in human hearts results in hatred, violence, murder, mass murder, and holocaust. Christians do well to remember that God created all people and that Jesus died for all people. Paul wrote that the Jews were his "kinsmen according to the flesh. They are Israelites, and to them belong the adoption, the glory, the covenants, the giving of the Law, the worship and the promises" (Romans 9:3–4). To harbor hatred for, to seek to harm, or to refuse to give aid to any person, Jew or Gentile, because of their ethnic or racial background is a sin.

God sent Jesus, the Son of a virgin Jewish mother, to be the Savior of all humankind. Jesus Himself said, "salvation is from the Jews" (John 4:22). Through faith in Him, Abraham is now also father of all those who believe (Romans 4:16–17). The Gospel "is the power of God for salvation to everyone who believes, to the Jew first and also to the Greek" (Romans 1:16). Christ has rescued us from sin, death, hell, and even hate. He is "the propitiation for our sins, and not for ours only but also for the sins of the whole world" (1 John 2:2). Indeed, God loves all people and has proven His love by offering up His one and only Son (John 3:16).

For All the Faithful Women

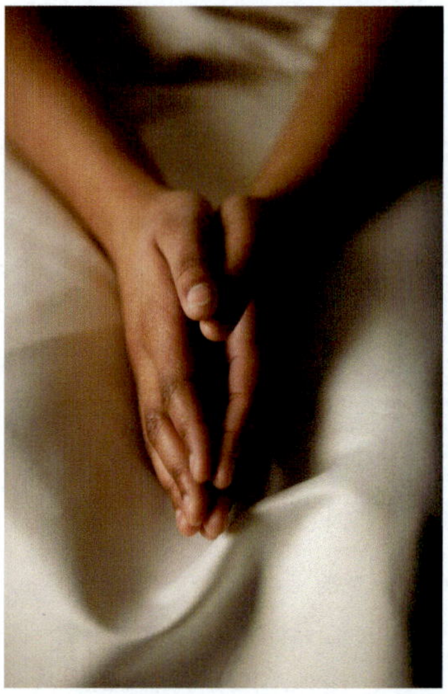

Perpetua and Felicitas are two women with two things in common. First, they were Christians living in Africa in the early part of the second century AD. Second, they died on the same day, martyred for their faith. In his book, *Fox's Book of Martyrs,* John Fox describes the martyrdom of Christian women, including Perpetua and Felicitas. These two faithful women suffered much on behalf of their Lord Jesus Christ before joining Him in His eternal kingdom. In spite of tremendous persecution, they remained faithful to God.

In 1993, a new hymn received its copyright. While the words of this hymn do not mention Perpetua and Felicitas by name, it certainly invokes them in spirit. The hymn, "For All the Faithful Women" appears in *Lutheran Service Book* (*LSB* 855). We take a moment to give thanks for all the women who in spite of difficulties and challenges remained faithful to God and His promises recorded in His Word. Some of their names are recorded in Scripture; others are listed in ancient or modern books. Many are those whom we know, while others may be known only to God.

Stanza One

For all the faithful women Who served in days of old,
To You shall thanks be given; To all, their story told.
They served with strength and gladness In tasks
Your wisdom gave.
To You their lives bore witness, Proclaimed Your pow'r to save.

Stanza Six

To Hannah, praying childless Before Your throne of grace,
You gave a son and called him To serve before Your face.
Grant us her perseverance; Lord, teach us how to pray
And trust in Your deliv'rance When darkness hides our way.
1 Samuel 1:1–2:10

Persevering Hannah, no children adorned your life. In your barrenness, you never forgot your Lord. Humbly, you knelt to pray. The desire of your prayer was that you might someday hold a child and hear the sweet cooing sound that only infants can make. In faith, you promised to give God any male child you bore. How difficult was it to take your son, newly weaned, and place him into Eli's hands (1 Samuel 1:24–28)? Did you know that your son would one day anoint David, Israel's greatest king? Did you know that through David your Messiah would one day come to save the world from its sins? You model for us sacrificial faith.

Stanza Seven

For Ruth, who left her homeland And ventured
forth in faith,
Who pledged to serve and worship Naomi's God
till death,
We praise You, God of Israel, And pray for hearts set free
To bind ourselves to others In love and loyalty.
Ruth 1:8–18

Faithful Ruth, your husband died and your mother-in-law sought to return to Israel. You, O creature of God, saw God's love reflected in Naomi's eyes and worked out through her hands. Leaving behind your family and your worthless idols, you acknowledged the Lord's handiwork by saying to Naomi, "Your people shall be my people, and your God my God" (Ruth 1:16). Gentle woman, God has honored you and your loyal faith by naming you in the lineage of Christ, one of only four women so named (Matthew 1:5).

Ruth Takes Away the Barley. James J. Tissot (1836–1902)

) ISTOCKPHOTO

Stanza Eight

We sing of Mary, mother, Fair maiden, full of grace.
She bore the Christ, our brother, Who came to save our race.
May we, with her, surrender Ourselves to Your command
And lay upon Your altar Our gifts of heart and hand.
Luke 1:26–38

Selfless Mary, mother of Jesus and thus God's mother, when the Lord's angel came near, you were afraid. Yet Gabriel's gentle words gave you courage, and you submitted to God's will and plan. "Behold," you said, "I am the servant of the Lord; let it be to me according to your word" (Luke 1:38). Thank you, heavenly Father, for allowing us to see in Mary's obedient faith, which was engendered and strengthened by Your Word, the Word that she heard with her ears and the Word made flesh that she by the Holy Spirit conceived and bore, our Jesus, our Savior.

Stanza Nine

We sing of busy Martha, Who toiled with pot and pan
While Mary sat in silence To hear the Word again.
Christ, keep our hearts attentive To truth that You declare,
And strengthen us for service When work becomes our prayer.
Luke 10:38–42

Busy Martha and attentive Mary, we recall the lesson that Jesus taught through you. Scurrying about, Martha, you remind us of ourselves. We never settle down long enough to hear God's Word, instead hurrying about in worldly persuits. Mary, you sat patiently at Jesus' feet, each word strengthening your soul. May we choose the "good portion" (Luke 10:42), the message of eternal life, and in receptive faith guard and keep it with all our hearts.

) SHUTTERSTOCK

Stanza Ten

Recall the outcast women With whom the Lord conversed;
Christ gave her living water To quench her deepest thirst.
Like her, our hearts are yearning; Christ offers us His Word.
Then may our lips be burning To witness to our Lord.
John 4:1–42

Dear woman at the well, our Savior's stop for cool water brought about your conversion. As the Lord spoke, you were convicted in your sin; your sin-parched soul ached for relief that only Jesus could bring. Dear Father in heaven, call to our minds the woman at the well as we repent of our sins, trust in Jesus alone for our salvation, and, like the woman at the well, tell others what Jesus has done for us. Grant us, like her, a sharing faith.

Stanza Eleven

We sing your praise for Mary, Who came at Easter dawn
To look for Jesus' body And found her Lord was gone.
But, as with joy she saw Him In resurrection light,
May we by faith behold Him, The Day who ends our night!
John 20:1–18

Forlorn Mary, whose Easter Sunday journey brought bittersweet tears. You thought that someone had stolen Christ's body and that your hurried goodbyes three days before must suffice. Then Christ's gentle "Mary" touches your heart. "I have seen the Lord!" you proclaim to the disciples (John 20:18). These same words echo through the mountains of time, not just on Easter, but every day of our lives—"He is risen!" "He is risen, indeed." Gracious Father, may we, like Mary, be filled with resurrection faith and joy!

Stanza Three

O God, for saints and servants, Those named and those unknown
In whom through all the ages Your light of glory shone,
We offer glad thanksgiving And fervent prayer we raise
That, faithful in Your service, Our lives may sing your praise.

Stanza Four

All praise to God the Father! All praise to Christ the Son!
All praise the Holy Spirit, Who binds the Church in one!
With saints who went before us, With saints who witness still,
We sing glad Alleluias And strive to do Your will.

© ISTOCKPHOTO

© SHUTTERSTOCK

Remain Faithful unto Death

We may not suffer martyrdom for our faith like Perpetua and Felicitas, but in this life we will suffer for our faith. Just as Jesus bore His cross, so, too, must we bear our crosses, whatever they may be. He said, "Whoever does not take his cross and follow Me is not worthy of Me" (Matthew 10:38). Disappointment, heartache, and grief will also affect us; we Christians are neither oblivious nor exempt from the effects of sin. Yet, in the midst of our trails and tribulations, Jesus commands us, "Be faithful unto death" (Revelation 2:10a).

But Jesus also says, "Whoever finds his life will lose it, and whoever loses his life for My sake will find it" (Matthew 10:39), and that He will give us the "crown of life" (Revelation 2:10b). Jesus died and rose again so that we may see and experience God's rich forgiveness in this present life and the joys of heaven in the next. "But you, beloved, building yourselves up in your most holy faith and praying in the Holy Spirit, keep yourselves in the love of God, waiting for the mercy of our Lord Jesus Christ that leads to eternal life" (Jude 20–21).

MORDECAI AND

MORDECAI BY JAMES TISSOT. © SUPERSTOCK, INC. / SUPERSTOCK

THE MESSIAH

THE SAVIOR BY JUAN DE JUANES. © ERICH LESSING / ART RESOURCE, NY.

When Matthew wrote His Gospel, he tailored his words for early Jewish Christians. No doubt these believers kept some of their Jewish traditions by celebrating the Festival of Purim every year. These men and women knew well the stories of their religious and cultural heritage. Just as you and I share the stories of our ancestors, the Jewish people recalled God's creation of the world, the fall of humankind into sin, and the promise of the coming Messiah. They also shared the stories of the patriarchs, Moses, the great judges of Israel, and her kings. But even further, they relayed the stories of God's grace in the lives of Ruth and Esther.

Steeped in tradition, including an important reference to the genealogy of Christ (Matthew 1:1–16), the Book of Matthew also relates some interesting parallels between the life of Mordecai and that of Jesus, the Messiah. You may be surprised to learn that in each of these six parallels, the life of Mordecai foreshadows the life of Jesus Christ.

False Worship

Mordecai refused to bow down to Haman, although King Ahasuerus had decreed it (Esther 3:1–3). When Mordecai's action came to Haman's attention, he intentionally appeared before Mordecai. Nevertheless, in keeping God's Word, Mordecai refused to offer worship to Haman. For Mordecai, honoring God's commandments was an important part of his daily life, as essential to life as breathing. The words of Exodus 20:3–5 meant more to Mordecai than life itself.

Jesus refused to bow down and worship the devil during the days of His temptation (Matthew 4:8–11). Following forty days of fasting, Jesus was at His weakest point, humanly speaking. The devil concluded his temptations by asking Jesus to "fall down and worship me" (v. 9). Instead of bowing down to the devil's command, our Lord stood up to Satan by quoting God's Holy Word, the source that Mordecai relied on while face-to-face with Haman.

A Royal Parade

Mordecai was honored with a public parade. After King Ahasuerus read how Mordecai had uncovered the assassination plot of Bigthan and Teresh, two of the king's eunuchs, he asked Haman, "What should be done to the man whom the king delights to honor?" (Esther 6:6). Thinking the honor for himself, evil Haman answered, "Let royal robes be brought, which the king has worn, and the horse that the king has ridden, and on whose head a royal crown is set. . . . Let them lead him on the horse through the square of the city" (vv. 8–9).

Although not on a stately horse, **Jesus** rode into Jerusalem on a donkey's back to shouts of acclamation, "Hosanna to the Son of David! Blessed is He who comes in the name of the Lord! Hosanna in the highest!" (Matthew 21:9). Later, shouts of honor would turn into jeers and demands for His crucifixion. Roman soldiers placed upon Him a scarlet robe, and thorns stood in place of Mordecai's crown (Matthew 27:27–31). In Matthew's account, we see the sad irony of this public honor, for Christ truly is a King.

MORDECAI'S TRIUMPH BY JAMES TISSOT © SUPERSTOCK, INC. / SUPERSTOCK

Blood Money

Haman's anger grew each time he considered how Mordecai refused to bend a knee to him. The Book of Esther brings the account of Haman's hatred toward Mordecai to a horrible climax: Haman's plot to have Mordecai hanged and the entire Jewish nation destroyed (Esther 3:6). To that end, Haman cast lots (the Pur) to determine the month that he would transfer his plan into reality (v. 7). Haman also offered to pay 10,000 talents of silver into King Ahasuerus's treasury if the king would allow him to destroy Mordecai and the Jews.

Jewish religious leaders, coveting their last vestige of political power, long plotted the death of Jesus. Judas Iscariot, one of Jesus' own disciples offered to betray Jesus. He asked them, "What will you give me if I deliver Him over to you?" Their quick response was 30 pieces of silver (Matthew 26:14–15). For a slave's ransom, Judas offered to betray the Savior of the world. In spite of this betrayal, God's plan of salvation marched forward to the cross. There Christ paid in full the ransom for the souls of humankind, His perfect life given in exchange for our tainted lives.

Wifely Warnings

Haman's wife, Zeresh, learned from her husband all about the incident of Mordecai's triumphant ride through the "square of the city" (Esther 6:9). Haman confessed his plot to destroy Mordecai and the Jews. In response, God issued a warning to Haman through his wife. "If Mordecai, before whom you have begun to fall," she warned, "is of the Jewish people, you will not overcome him but will surely fall before him" (v. 13). Ignoring his wife, the prideful Haman continued to pursue the path that led to his own downfall.

Pilate's wife also warned her husband. While Jesus stood before Pontius Pilate, she sent Pilate a note. Reading the small piece of paper, Pilate read, "Have nothing to do with that righteous man, for I have suffered much because of Him today in a dream" (Matthew 27:19). As Haman had done, Pilate ignored his wife and handed Jesus over for crucifixion. Although Pilate "washed his hands" of Jesus' innocent murder (v. 24), Pilate remains immortalized in the words of the Apostles' Creed.

Hanging Enemies

The fate **Haman** devised for Mordecai ultimately became his own. The gallows constructed to stand some 70 feet tall (50 cubits, according to Esther 5:14) was used by King Ahasuerus to hang Haman (Esther 7:10). At Esther's request, Haman's ten sons received the same fate as their father (Esther 9:13–14), perhaps serving as a warning to those who would persecute the Jews.

In shame for betraying Jesus, **Judas** took his own life by hanging (Matthew 27:3–10). Even "throwing down the pieces of silver into the temple" (Matthew 27:5) could not assuage Judas's shame. As with Haman, the evil Judas intended became God's instrument of salvation for His people, and later, through Christ, the salvation of all.

Ultimate Victory

For **Mordecai**, all the power and authority once belonging to Haman became his. The signet ring Haman wore found a new home on Mordecai's hand. Queen Esther "set Mordecai over the house of Haman" (Esther 8:2). Royal robes adorned Mordecai, while a golden crown sat on his brow (Esther 8:15–17). The Jews remember Mordecai's victory through an annual celebration known as Purim (for more information, see "The Feast of Purim" on page 14 in this enrichment magazine).

Christ's victory was enacted in His death and resurrection. While Mordecai's victory was over one man, Haman, Jesus' death and resurrection conquered sin, death, and the devil (Matthew 28:1–10; 16–20). As Christians, we celebrate this great victory each time we gather around the Lord's Table for the feast we know as the Lord's Supper. Paul, the evangelist, says, "For as often as you eat this bread and drink this cup, you proclaim the Lord's death until He comes" (1 Corinthians 11:26).

Mordecai Points Us to Christ

The devil and our sinful flesh continually work to make us more like Haman than Mordecai. Our sinfulness merits only death for you and me. We cannot rely on ourselves for salvation. Our state is hopeless.

By God's hand, Mordecai and Esther saved the Jewish people from extermination. Yet to fully appreciate their achievement, we must look further to Jesus' bloody cross and His empty tomb. There He won an even more astounding victory. God's only Son died for the sins of all humankind, and on the third day He rose again for our justification. By God's grace, Jesus' victory is ours!

Kindred Spirits

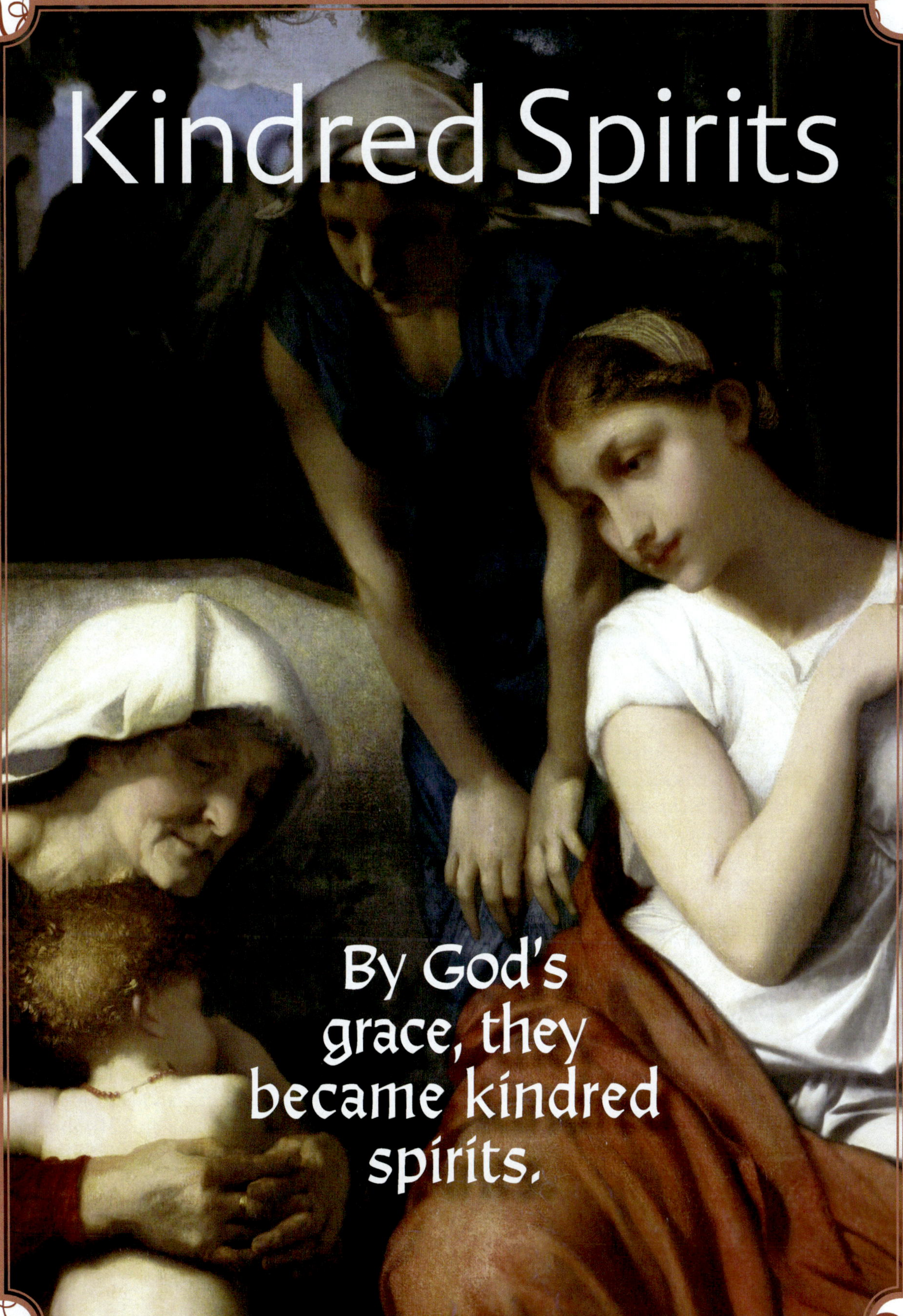

By God's grace, they became kindred spirits.

In *Saying Grace*, artist Norman Rockwell depicts an older woman and a young boy sitting at a restaurant table with bowed heads. Sharing the table are two young men. They stare in reverent wonder as grandmother and grandson pray. *Saying Grace* adorned the cover of an issue of the *Saturday Evening Post*, one of many Rockwell paintings to do so, and it remains one of this author's many favorites.

We can easily image a similar scene in the lives of Naomi and Ruth, can't we? Perhaps Naomi led the prayers as she and Ruth gathered for a meal. Their gentle walks together, their common prayers, their mutual conversations, their shared grief, and their shared joy—all of these things brought Naomi and Ruth closer to each other. By God's grace, they became kindred spirits.

As Christians, you and I are kindred spirits brought about by our fellowship with Christ. In fellowship with God through our faith in Jesus, we have fellowship with one another. Naomi and Ruth model for all believers the fellowship we enjoy by God's grace.

Fellowship with God

We often associate *fellowship* with donuts and coffee between worship services or perhaps even the church potluck. However, this type of fellowship isn't the same as the fellowship we enjoy as believers. As Christ's body, we share a special fellowship with God through Jesus' death and resurrection (Ephesians 2:4–7). Out of this spiritual unity with our heavenly Father arises a fellowship that believers share with each other (1 John 1:7).

Early Christians referred to this relationship as *koinonia* (Greek for "to share in, fellowship with, or participate"). Believers do not create this fellowship; rather, it is received as a gift. Jesus' death and resurrection achieved this fellowship for us: "I in them and You in Me, that they may become perfectly one, so that the world may know that You sent Me and loved them even as You loved Me" (John 17:23). The fellowship that we enjoy with God through faith in Christ is beyond human comprehension.

Fellowship with Fellow Believers

Besides fellowship with God, believers also share another common fellowship with each another. James urges Christians to confess their sins to one another and to pray for one another (James 5:16). The giving of their tithes and offerings constitutes another way believers fellowship with one another. These gifts "contribute to the needs of the saints [their fellow forgiven sinners] and seek to show hospitality" (Romans 12:13).

With the Holy Spirit's guidance, Christians also learn to bear one another's faults while learning to please others (Romans 15:1, 2). They share in each other's sufferings and work to gently restore those whose faith may be weak (Galatians 6:1–2). They share a mutual interest in one another, including their spiritual well-being (Hebrews 13:16). Love for one another makes up one side of the coin of life. Fellowship makes up the other (1 John 4:12).

In Holy Communion, believers fellowship with God and with each other in a most intimate way, namely through Christ's body and blood (1 Corinthians 11:25–26). We "participate" in Christ's body and blood (1 Corinthians 10:16) and through faith receive the benefits of His atoning work through this holy meal. We enjoy *koinonia* with Jesus' true body and His true blood. At the same time, we are also one body with fellow communicants (v. 17) and even with believers already in heaven.

Fellowship: A Gift of God's Love

John warns, "If we say we have fellowship with Him while we walk in darkness, we lie and do not practice the truth" (1 John 1:6). In other words, we may have fellowship with others while we continue in our sin, but we do not have fellowship with God. Without fellowship with God through faith in Christ, we are utterly lost. We are in danger of spending an eternity in hell. That is a terrible thought.

Nevertheless John also wrote, "If we walk in the light [repent of our sins, and seek God's forgiveness through Christ], as He is in the light, we have fellowship with one another, and the blood of Jesus His Son cleanses us from all sin" (1 John 1:7). In Christ, we have the assurance of God's forgiveness and His eternal fellowship. Like the praying pair in Rockwell's *Saying Grace*, we give thanks. We give thanks that "God is faithful, by whom [we] were called into the fellowship of His Son, Jesus Christ our Lord" (1 Corinthians 1:9).

Study Guide

LifeLight Expands

LifeLight

Available NOW!

The Bible: An Overview
Genesis, Pt. 1
Genesis, Pt. 2
Exodus, Pt. 1
Exodus, Pt. 2
Wilderness Wanderings
Joshua
Judges
Ruth/Esther
1 & 2 Samuel
Life of David
1 & 2 Kings
1 & 2 Chronicles

Ezra/Nehemiah
Job
Selected Psalms
Proverbs
Ecclesiastes/
Song of Solomon
Isaiah, Pt. 1
Isaiah, Pt. 2
Jeremiah/Lamentations
Ezekiel
Daniel
Hosea/Joel/Amos
Obadiah/Jonah/Micah
Minor Prophets

Nahum/Habakkuk/
Zephaniah
Haggai/Zechariah/
Malachi
Matthew, Pt. 1
Matthew, Pt. 2
Mark
Luke, Pt. 1
Luke, Pt. 2
John, Pt. 1
John, Pt. 2
Acts, Pt. 1
Acts, Pt. 2

Romans, Pt. 1
Romans, Pt. 2
1 Corinthians
2 Corinthians
Galatians/Philippians/
Colossians
Ephesians/
1 & 2 Thessalonians
Timothy/Titus/Philemon
Hebrews
James/Jude
1 & 2 Peter
1, 2, 3 John
Revelation

LifeLight Foundations

Baptism
Bible Feasts
Creation, New Creation
The Christian's Mission

End Times
Heaven & Hell
Law & Gospel
Ministry

Miracles
Parables
Prayer
Prophecy

Time between the
Testaments
Triune God
Worship

Women of the Bible

Distribute before session 1 for use in session 1.
Use enrichment magazine pp. 2–4.

Genesis 1:26–27; 2:22–23; 1 Peter 3:5–7

Resources for Worship

Use these resources for your daily study at home and at the week's assembly.

Hymn

Christ, the life of all the living,
Christ, the death of death, our foe,
Who, Thyself for me once giving
To the darkest depths of woe:
Through Thy suff'rings, death, and merit
I eternal life inherit.
Thousand, thousand thanks shall be,
Dearest Jesus, unto Thee.

Thou hast suffered great affliction
And hast borne it patiently,
Even death by crucifixion,
Fully to atone for me;
Thou didst choose to be tormented
That my doom should be prevented.
Thousand, thousand thanks shall be,
Dearest Jesus, unto Thee.

Then, for all that wrought my pardon,
For Thy sorrows deep and sore,
For Thine anguish in the Garden,
I will thank Thee evermore,
Thank Thee for Thy groaning, sighing,
For Thy bleeding and Thy dying,
For that last triumphant cry,
And shall praise Thee, Lord, on high.

Ernst Christoph Homburg, 1605–81; tr. Catherine Winkworth, 1827–78, sts. 1 and 3, alt.;
tr. *Evangelical Lutheran Hymn-Book*, St. Louis, 1912, st. 2 (*LSB* 420; *LW* 94; *TLH* 151; *LBW* 97; *CW* 114; *ELH* 333; *EVaS* disk 3, track 11).

Prayer

Almighty God, our most gracious heavenly Father, teach us by Your Holy Spirit, whom You have poured out upon us in Baptism. Grant us hearing ears and believing hearts to receive the good things of Your blessed Word, which alone can infallibly guide us into all truth, through Jesus Christ, Your Son, our Savior and Brother, who lives and reigns with You and the Holy Spirit, one God, now and forever. Amen.

Digging Deep
My Personal Study for Week 1

Day 1 • Read Genesis 1 and 2

1. The record of Genesis is the divine witness (the truth) of the origin of the universe. In six days, God created the universe, with humankind His crowning achievement. (See Genesis 1:26–27.)

a. What is humankind's position in relation to the earthly creation?

b. What characterizes the humans to whom authority is given?

2. Genesis 1 gives a general or summary account of creation, telling of the basic fact and nature of the universe's (and humankind's) existence. In Genesis 2, the Holy Spirit gives specific and crucial details of humanity's creation in particular. God created the man and the woman in different ways. How was each created?

3. In Genesis 2:22, we are told that God "brought [the woman] to the man." Why was this significant?

4. The woman was the last of all God's creation. Why does this make her special? Read Proverbs 31:10–31, especially verse 28; Luke 9:48; and Revelation 21:1–5, 9–10.

Day 2 • Read Genesis 3 and 1 Timothy 2:11–15

5. When and to whom did God give the command not to eat of the tree of the knowledge of good and evil? See Genesis 2:16–17.

6. **Challenge question:** Consider the strategy of the serpent (Satan) in approaching the woman. (See 2 Corinthians 11:3 and Revelation 12:9.) How did he succeed in getting her to eat the forbidden fruit? How does this sort of thing happen in our world today?

7. Sin brought with it God's judgment. Yet in Genesis 3:15, God promised that the Seed of the woman, Jesus Christ, would crush the serpent's head. The serpent would succeed only in bruising the "heel" of the woman's Seed. How has God turned the tables on the devil, sin, death, and hell by promising and then bringing salvation through Eve's Seed?

8. Why did Adam call Eve "the mother of all living"? What is Eve's part in the promise and its fulfillment? In what way is she a model and expression of the Christian Church?

9. When Eve gave birth to her first son, she said, "I have gotten a Man, the LORD" (English translation of Luther). In what way was she right, and in what way was she wrong?

Day 3 • Read Luke 1:26–45

10. After thousands of years of human history, God made good on His promise to provide the world's Savior, the woman's Seed. By the power of the Holy Spirit, the Virgin Mary was made to conceive the very Son of God.

a. In Luke 1:26–38, what things were said about Mary's child that reveal His identity?

God's Loving Faithfulness

Distribute before session 2 for use in session 2.
Use enrichment magazine pp. 5–7.

Ruth 1

Resources for Worship

Use these resources for your daily study at home and at the week's assembly.

Hymn

The Lord's my shepherd, I'll not want;
He makes me down to lie
In pastures green; He leadeth me
The quiet waters by.

My soul He doth restore again
And me to walk doth make
Within the paths of righteousness,
E'en for His own name's sake.

Yea, though I walk in death's dark vale,
Yet will I fear no ill;
For Thou art with me, and Thy rod
And staff me comfort still.

My table Thou hast furnished
In presence of my foes;
My head Thou dost with oil anoint,
And my cup overflows.

Goodness and mercy all my life
Shall surely follow me;
And in God's house forevermore
My dwelling place shall be.

The Psalms of David in Meeter, Edinburgh, 1650 (*LSB* 710; *LW* 416; *TLH* 436; *LBW* 451; *CW* 360; *ELH* 371; *EVaS* disk 9, track 14).

Prayer

Almighty God, our most gracious heavenly Father, we praise You for choosing and using things despised by this world and so displaying Your glory. Through Holy Scripture, continue to give us poor sinners the Gospel of a Savior who was despised and thought nothing by the world. Grant us the spirit of wisdom to see in the divinely inspired words of Ruth this good news of Your mercy in Jesus Christ, in whose name we pray. Amen.

Digging Deep
My Personal Study for Week 2

Day 1 • Read Ruth 4:17–22

1. We begin with the end of Ruth to see where its narrative leads us. Jewish tradition ascribed the human authorship of Ruth to Samuel. Why does the mention of David in this brief genealogy suggest otherwise? See 1 Samuel 25:1; 2 Samuel 2:4; and 5:3–5.

2. This genealogy covers a period of about nine centuries.

a. How many ancestors of David does it list?

b. Is it plausible that this brief genealogy highlights certain individuals without naming every descendent in the line? Why?

c. Who was Perez? (See Genesis 38:1–29.) Why would this genealogy at the end of Ruth start with him?

3. How were people saved in Old Testament times? See Acts 10:43 and Hebrews 11:7.

4. Based on the following passages, calculate the time span recorded in the Book of Ruth:

Ruth 1:4________________

Ruth 1:22; 2:23 ________________

Ruth 4:1–22 ________________

Total ____________________

Day 2 • Reading assignments are in each question

5. The narrative of Ruth unfolds in four major parts. Briefly summarize each of these parts according to the following passages:

a. 1:6–18

b. 2:1–17

c. 3:6–15

d. 4:1–12

6. **Challenge question:** Describe the introduction and the conclusion (or epilogue) to Ruth (Ruth 1:1–5 and 4:13–22). What might these sections tell a reader who knows nothing else about this story?

7. Identify the main people in this story in the order they appear. What people are mentioned in 4:11–12, and what purpose do they serve?

Day 3 • Reading assignments are in each question

8. The events of Ruth took place at the time of the judges.

a. Read Judges 2, and briefly summarize the conflict and experience of the Israelites at that time.

b. What would the Israelites have thought about the Moabites, and why? Read Genesis 19:30–38; Numbers 22:1–6; 31:15–16; and Judges 3:12–14.

The Act of Redemption

Distribute before session 3 for use in session 3.
Use enrichment magazine pp. 8–10.

Ruth 2

Resources for Worship

Use these resources for your daily study at home and at the week's assembly.

Hymn

How sweet the name of Jesus sounds
In a believer's ear!
It soothes our sorrows, heals our wounds,
And drives away our fear.

It makes the wounded spirit whole
And calms the heart's unrest;
'Tis manna to the hungry soul
And to the weary, rest.

Dear name! The rock on which I build,
My shield and hiding place;
My never-failing treasury filled
With boundless stores of grace.

O Jesus, shepherd, guardian, friend,
My Prophet, Priest, and King,
My Lord, my life, my way, my end,
Accept the praise I bring.

How weak the effort of my heart,
How cold my warmest thought!
But when I see Thee as Thou art,
I'll praise Thee as I ought.

Till then I would Thy love proclaim
With ev'ry fleeting breath;
And may the music of Thy name
Refresh my soul in death!

John Newton, 1725–1807, alt.
(*LSB* 524; *LW* 279; *TLH* 364; *LBW* 345; *CW* 358; *ELH* 155; *EVaS* disk 6, track 23).

Prayer

Almighty God, our most gracious heavenly Father, we thank You for Your abundant mercy in Jesus Christ, by whose resurrection we have been born again and made heirs of the living hope of eternal life. Though we were estranged from You by sin, You showed us Your loving-kindness and reconciled us to Yourself by the blood of the cross. Grant us to hear Your Word today with believing ears and hearts, through Jesus Christ, Your Son, our Savior, who lives and reigns with You and the Holy Spirit, one God, now and forever. Amen.

Digging Deep
My Personal Study for Week 3

Day 1 • Read Ruth 1:1–18

1. Read Ruth 1:1–5. The story of Ruth begins with the departure from Israel by Elimilech (el IM el EK) and his family and their settling in Moab. Why did Elimelech leave the land of Israel? Did he intend to live in Moab permanently?

2. After the death of her husband and sons, Naomi returned to Israel, having heard that the famine there had ended. What twofold blessing did Naomi invoke upon her two daughters-in-law (vv. 8 and 9)? Why did she ask her daughters-in-law to leave? Share how your experiences of particular mercies from God have made you sensitive to the needs of others.

3. Although Orpah returned home, Ruth "clung" to Naomi (1:14). She insisted on remaining with her mother-in-law. Now, rather than receiving strangers

(as she did with Naomi's family when they came to Moab, even accepting marriage to Mahlon [4:10]), Ruth would be received as a stranger in a new land. What did Naomi say to show Ruth's hospitality (1:8)? Why is it appropriate that *Ruth* perhaps means "friendship"?

4. **Challenge question:** Discuss Ruth's pledge in 1:16–17. In what five things did she pledge to join Naomi? How can Naomi remind us of Christ?

Day 2 • Read Ruth 1:19–2:23

5. Upon return to Bethlehem with Ruth, what name did Naomi ask to be called?

6. It was "the beginning of barley harvest" (1:22). Ruth gleaned, that is, retrieved leftovers in the grain fields. (See Leviticus 19:9–10; 23:22; and Deuteronomy 24:19–21.) How did she end up gleaning in the plot that belonged to Boaz, a wealthy relative of Naomi's late husband (2:3)? How does this development underscore the grace of God in this story?

7. List four things about Boaz from Ruth 2 that show him to be a man of grace and good character.

a. Verse 4

b. Verse 9

c. Verse 11

d. Verses 14–19

8. Describe how Ruth may have felt about being treated so kindly and generously, even though she was an outsider? How does this picture God's kindness to us?

9. How did Boaz characterize Ruth's faith? Compare Psalm 17:8; 36:7; and 57:1.

10. Naomi learned that Ruth gleaned in the fields of Boaz.

a. What did Naomi say about God when she told Ruth that Boaz was one of their redeemers (Ruth 2:20)?

Esther Becomes Queen

Distribute before session 4 for use in session 4.
Use enrichment magazine pp. 11–13.

Esther 1:1–2:18

Resources for Worship

Use these resources for your daily study at home and at the week's assembly.

Hymn

Jesus shall reign where'er the sun
Does its successive journeys run;
His kingdom stretch from shore to shore
Till moons shall wax and wane no more.

To Him shall endless prayer be made,
And endless praises crown His head;
His name like sweet perfume shall rise
With ev'ry morning sacrifice.

People and realms of ev'ry tongue
Dwell on His love with sweetest song;
And infant voices shall proclaim
Their early blessings on His name.

Blessings abound where'er He reigns:
The pris'ners leap, unloose their chains,
The weary find eternal rest,
And all who suffer want are blest.

Let ev'ry creature rise and bring
Honors peculiar to our King;
Angels descend with songs again,
And earth repeat the loud amen.

Isaac Watts, 1674–1748, alt.
(*LSB* 832; *LW* 312; *TLH* 511; *LBW* 530; *CW* 84; *ELH* 193; *EVaS* disk 7, track 13).

Prayer

Almighty God, our most gracious heavenly Father, Your ways are unsearchable and Your paths untraceable. Yet You have revealed to us in the Gospel that in and with Your Son, Jesus Christ, You are present everywhere, working through Him the triumph of His salvation for Your people. Though we cannot know this with our reason or detect this by our senses, we confess it to be true according to Your Word, and we ask that You would build up our faith in this hidden reality, through Jesus Christ, Your Son, our Lord, who lives and reigns with You and the Holy Spirit, one God, now and forever. Amen.

Digging Deep
My Personal Study for Week 4

Day 1 • Reading assignments are in each question

1. Esther is set in the Persian Kingdom during the reign of Ahasuerus (Xerxes, who ruled 486–465 BC). Jews were living in various places since they had been forcibly deported from Judah by the previous dominant empire, Babylon. Read Daniel 1:1–6. What sorts of deportees did the Babylonians single out to be set aside for royal service?

2. The deportee Daniel gained high rank among counselors to the kings of both Babylon and Medo-Persia. After the Lord kept Daniel safe in the lions' den, what decree did the Persian ruler make? See Daniel 6:25–28.

3. Cyrus was the Persian king who defeated the Babylonians more than fifty years before the events of the Book of Esther. What did he decree in Ezra 1:1–4?

4. *Skim through* the Book of Esther and count the number of times you find the name of God or any reference to Him. Discuss the significance of your findings.

Day 2 • Read Esther 1:1–12

5. King Ahasuerus held a state banquet in his palace at Susa, one of four capital cities in the empire.

a. Who is said to have attended this festival?

b. What was Ahasuerus's purpose in holding this great banquet?

6. How long was this banquet?

7. A second feast of seven days followed. This one was held for all those who served in the citadel.

a. Describe the opulence of this feast.

b. What order was given in 1:8?

8. What other feast took place at this time?

9. Queen Vashti was summoned to Ahasuerus's feast on the seventh (and final) day. How did she respond?

Day 3 • Read Esther 1:12–22

10. The king was humiliated and left seething in his anger (1:12). He convened a meeting with his most trusted officials to determine how he should respond to Vashti's public effrontery. How do verses 13 and 14 describe those summoned to the council?

11. Vashti was deposed and forbidden from ever coming "before King Ahasuerus." How was this decree made permanent according to 1:19? (See also 3:12–14; 8:8–14; and Daniel 6:8.)

Haman's Plot against the Jews

Distribute before session 5 for use in session 5.
Use enrichment magazine pp. 14–17.

Esther 2:19–3:15

Resources for Worship

Use these resources for your daily study at home and at the week's assembly.

Hymn

Lord, keep us steadfast in Your Word;
Curb those who by deceit or sword
Would wrest the kingdom from Your Son
And bring to naught all He has done.

Lord Jesus Christ, Your pow'r make known,
For You are Lord of lords alone;
Defend Your holy Church that we
May sing Your praise eternally.

O Comforter of priceless worth,
Send peace and unity on earth;
Support us in our final strife
And lead us out of death to life.

Martin Luther 1483–1546; tr. Catherine Winkworth, 1827–78, alt. (*LSB* 655; *LW* 334; *TLH* 261; *LBW* 230; *CW* 203; *ELH* 589; *EVaS* disk 5, track 13).

Prayer

Almighty God, our heavenly Father, without Your help our labor is useless, and without Your light our search is in vain. Invigorate our study of Your holy Word that, by due diligence and right discernment, we may establish ourselves and others in Your holy faith; through Jesus Christ, our Lord. Amen. (*LSB*, p. 312)

Digging Deep
My Personal Study for Week 5

Day 1 • Read Esther 2:19–23

1. Esther's obedience to Mordecai is noted in this section. Why? How does it become important?

2. Mordecai learned of a conspiracy against Ahasuerus by two palace guards, Bigthan and Teresh (2:21). He relayed this information to Esther, who reported it to the king. What happened as a result of the conspiracy being exposed? What was the method of punishment?

3. Mordecai did not receive any initial reward for helping to save the king's life. How does Galatians 6:9 encourage us to live God-pleasing lives even though we may see no benefits in this world?

4. List ways in which we, as citizens, can show regard for those in authority. How can we allow political party affiliation to prejudice us and create bias?

Day 2 • Read Esther 3:1

5. In Esther 3:1, we are introduced to a man named Haman, who is identified as "the Agagite, the son of Hammedatha."

a. Read Exodus 17:8–16 and Deuteronomy 25:17–19. How were the Israelites to view the Amalekites?

b. Read 1 Samuel 15:1–33. Note that the Amalekite king was named Agag. After the events of 1 Samuel 15, what do you suppose was the attitude of the Amalekites (possibly relatives of this Agag) toward Israelites and maybe Jews (those of the Southern Kingdom, Judah) in particular?

6. To what position was Haman appointed?

7. To the Jews, this was as if their mortal enemy had become king.

a. Was this a sign that God was against them? Should they have seen this as a rejection?

b. When we see cases of the wicked being exalted and others wrongfully passed by, how can promises such as Romans 8:28; Isaiah 55:8–9; and Psalm 73 be of comfort to us?

Day 3 • Read Esther 3:2–6

8. The royal servants "who were at the king's gate" paid homage to Haman by bowing down in his presence. Why did Mordecai not show obeisance to Haman?

9. How can Mordecai's stubborn resistance be a model for our response? How might it be misused?

Esther Intercedes

Distribute before session 6 for use in session 6.
Use enrichment magazine pp. 18–21.

Esther 4:1–5:8

Resources for Worship

Use these resources for your daily study at home and at the week's assembly.

Hymn

A mighty fortress is our God,
  A trusty shield and weapon;
He helps us free from ev'ry need
  That hath us now o'ertaken.
The old evil foe
Now means deadly woe;
  Deep guile and great might
  Are his dread arms in fight;
On earth is not his equal.

With might of ours can naught be done,
  Soon were our loss effected;
But for us fights the valiant One,
  Whom God Himself elected.
Ask ye, Who is this?
Jesus Christ it is,
  Of Sabaoth Lord,
  And there's none other God;
He holds the field forever.

Though devils all the world should fill,
  All eager to devour us,
We tremble not, we fear no ill;
  They shall not overpow'r us.
This world's prince may still
Scowl fierce as he will,
  He can harm us none.
  He's judged; the deed is done;
One little word can fell him.

The Word they still shall let remain
  Nor any thanks have for it;
He's by our side upon the plain
  With His good gifts and Spirit.
And take they our life,
Goods, fame, child, and wife,
  Though these all be gone,
  Our vict'ry has been won;
The Kingdom ours remaineth.

Martin Luther, 1483–1546; tr. composite.

(*LSB* 657; *LW* 297; *LBW* 229; *CW* 201; *ELH* 250/251; *EVaS* disk 7, track 10).

Prayer

O God and Father of our Lord Jesus Christ, who sustained Him in His hour of trial and provided deliverance out of death, raising Him to life immortal, fortify our hearts with Your promises of the same, creating and confirming faith in us always by Your Spirit working through the Gospel. In Jesus' name we ask it. Amen.

Digging Deep
My Personal Study for Week 6

Day 1 • Read Esther 4:1–3

1. The edict's gruesome order impacted the whole city and deeply affected the Jewish population. How did the Jews react to the public order for their destruction (a genocidal pogrom), according to 4:1–3?

2. The Book of Esther does not mention God. Here, how does it refer to Him without mentioning His name?

3. What kind of fear does Luke 12:4–5 counsel us to have?

4. How did the Jews demonstrate such fear? How might we?

Day 2 • Read Esther 4:2

5. **Challenge question:** Consider the larger biblical teaching about fasting. In fasting, we set aside time for exclusive consideration and contemplation of God and our lives before Him. It may be occasioned by tragedy, trial, temptation, or even worship (preparation for the Lord's Supper). It involves abstaining from food (not water) for a specified time to focus upon prayer and meditation on God's Word.

a. Does fasting in and of itself have any spiritual benefit? Is it a discipline of the flesh?

b. What instructions did Christ give on fasting in Matthew 6:16?

c. What do you think Jesus meant in Luke 5:34–35?

6. List ways in which fasting has been misused and mistaught in the Christian Church.

7. Why do you suppose the king forbade people to enter his gate in sackcloth?

8. How does this differ from the way God treats us?

Day 3 • Read Esther 4:4–11

9. Esther learned of Mordecai's behavior. What effect did this have on her? Why?

10. Complete the following sentences based on Esther 4:4–9.

a. Mordecai refused to take off the

____.

b. Hathach met Mordecai in the ________________

________ of the city in front of the _______________.

Mordecai Up, Haman Down

Distribute before session 7 for use in session 7.
Use enrichment magazine pp. 22–25.

Esther 5:9–7:10

Resources for Worship

Use these resources for your daily study at home and at the week's assembly.

Hymn

How firm a foundation, O saints of the Lord,
Is laid for your faith in His excellent Word!
What more can He say than to you He has said
Who unto the Savior for refuge have fled?

"Fear not! I am with you, O be not dismayed,
For I am your God and will still give you aid;
I'll strengthen you, help you, and cause you to
stand,
Upheld by My righteous, omnipotent hand.

"The soul that on Jesus has leaned for repose
I will not, I will not, desert to his foes;
That soul, though all hell should endeavor to
shake,
I'll never, no never, no never, forsake!

"When through fiery trials your pathway will lie,
My grace, all-sufficient, will be your supply.
The flames will not hurt you; I only design
Your dross to consume and your gold to refine.

"Throughout all their lifetime My people will
prove
My sov'reign, eternal, unchangeable love;
And then, when gray hairs will their temples
adorn,
Like lambs they will still in My bosom be
borne."

A Selection of Hymns, London, 1787, alt.
(*LSB* 728; *LW* 411; *TLH* 427; *LBW* 507; *CW* 416; *ELH* 521; *EVaS* disk 9, track 12).

Prayer

O gracious heavenly Father, we thank You that You are our refuge in times of trial and suffering. By the power of Your Son's Passion and death on the cross, You have triumphed over all that is adverse to us and subdued all our enemies, making their plans and works serve Your own good and saving will. By the divine mercy in Jesus Christ through which You justify the ungodly and bless sinners, grant to us now the mind of the Spirit so that we may behold the wondrous things of our salvation, through Jesus Christ, Your Son, our Lord, who lives and reigns with You and the Holy Spirit, one God, now and forever. Amen.

Digging Deep
My Personal Study for Week 7

Day 1 • Read Esther 5:9–14

1. Haman started home from Queen Esther's private banquet in a state of euphoria. However, his mood quickly changed when he passed Mordecai at the king's gate.

a. How does verse 9 describe Haman's mood change?

b. What did Mordecai do that provoked Haman?

2. List the four things that Haman recounted to his wife and friends.

a.

b.

c.

d.

3. In verse 12, what did Haman boast of beyond these?

4. Despite all this, Haman remained dissatisfied because of "Mordecai the Jew sitting at the king's gate." His wife, Zeresh, and his friends proposed that he build a gallows 50 cubits high (approximately 75 feet) and hang (impale) Mordecai on it.

a. How did this idea strike Haman? Why?

b. Why do you think Haman had not had Mordecai executed until now?

c. Why do you think it enrages those who use threats, intimidation, and bullying when their tactics are resisted? What does Romans 8:31–39 counsel?

Day 2 • Read Esther 6:1–11

5. Troubled by insomnia, King Ahasuerus called for the "book of memorable deeds" to be brought and read before him. He discovered that Mordecai was never honored for his loyalty to the king in exposing an assassination plot.

a. What do you think is the connection between the king's restlessness and the "book of memorable deeds"?

b. How was God's hand at work here?

6. Before deciding what honors to bestow upon Mordecai, the king noticed someone in the court. Learning it was Haman, the king summoned him and asked his advice on how to treat the man "whom the king delights to honor."

a. Why had Haman come to the king?

b. Why did Haman believe the king was referring to him?

7. What did Haman recommend be done for the man whom the king wished to honor?

The Curse Reversed

Distribute before session 8 for use in session 8.
Use enrichment magazine pp. 26–30.

Esther 8:1–9:19

Resources for Worship

Use these resources for your daily study at home and at the week's assembly.

Hymn

Lord of glory, You have bought us
With Your lifeblood as the price,
Never grudging for the lost ones
That tremendous sacrifice;
And with that have freely given
Blessings countless as the sand
To the unthankful and the evil
With Your own unsparing hand.

Grant us hearts, dear Lord, to give You
Gladly, freely of Your own.
With the sunshine of Your goodness
Melt our thankless hearts of stone
Till our cold and selfish natures,
Warmed by You, at length believe
That more happy and more blessed
'Tis to give than to receive.

Wondrous honor You have given
To our humblest charity
In Your own mysterious sentence,
"You have done it all to Me."
Can it be, O gracious Master,
That You deign for alms to sue,
Saying by Your poor and needy,
"Give as I have giv'n to you"?

Lord of glory, You have bought us
With Your lifeblood as the price,
Never grudging for the lost ones
That tremendous sacrifice.
Give us faith to trust You boldly,
Hope, to stay our souls on You;
But, oh, best of all Your graces,
With Your love our love renew.

Eliza S. Alderson, 1818–89, alt.
(*LSB* 815; *LW* 402; *TLH* 442; *LBW* 424; *CW* 486; *ELH* 459; *EVaS* disk 9, track 9).

Prayer

Righteous Father, we thank You that You have won for us, through Your Son's own obedience, eternal life and victory over sin and the grave. Help us now as we once again hear and contemplate so great a salvation and believe it firmly for ourselves; through Jesus Christ, Your Son, our Lord, who lives and reigns with You and the Holy Spirit, one God, now and forever. Amen.

Digging Deep
My Personal Study for Week 8

Day 1 • Read Esther 8:1–14

1. Esther 8:1 and 2 begins the anticlimactic portion of Esther. Haman's house and property were given to Esther, and his office and privileges were given to Mordecai.

a. What specific action was taken by the king to vest Mordecai with Haman's position?

b. What did Esther then do for Mordecai?

2. **Challenge question:** Following this, Esther again fell down before the king in a plea for mercy. After he extended the golden scepter, she requested a revocation of the decree to destroy the Jews.

a. Unlike earlier, why was Esther not fearful to approach the king this time?

b. How did the king respond? Why wasn't his previous decree revoked? How can these events put you in mind of the distinction between Law and Gospel?

3. According to 8:9, how long after the original edict was the second one given?

4. How did the thirteenth day of Adar become a good one for the Jews? How did God's use of it help the triumph of faith over superstition?

Day 2 • Read Esther 8:15–17

5. Verse 15 shifts to a scene in which Mordecai was leaving the king's presence arrayed in royal garments.

a. Did the colors and material of Mordecai's robe resemble colors mentioned elsewhere in Esther? Where?

b. What else did he wear?

6. How does the public's reaction differ from its reaction in 3:15?

7. Contrast the Jews' state of being in 8:16 with that described in 4:3, 16. Fill in the following table:

4:3, 16	8:16

A Reason to Celebrate

Distribute before session 9 for use in session 9.
Use enrichment magazine pp. 31–32.

Esther 9:20–10:3

Resources for Worship

Use these resources for your daily study at home and at the week's assembly.

Hymn

Now thank we all our God
With hearts and hands and voices,
Who wondrous things has done,
In whom His world rejoices;
Who from our mothers' arms
Has blest us on our way
With countless gifts of love
And still is ours today.

Oh, may this bounteous God
Through all our life be near us,
With ever joyful hearts
And blessèd peace to cheer us
And keep us in His grace
And guide us when perplexed
And free us from all ills
In this world and the next!

All praise and thanks to God
The Father now be given,
The Son, and Him who reigns
With them in highest heaven,
The one eternal God,
Whom earth and heav'n adore;
For thus it was, is now,
And shall be evermore.

Martin Rinckart, 1586–1649; tr. Catherine Winkworth, 1827–78, alt.
(*LSB* 895; *LW* 443; *TLH* 36; *LBW* 533; *CW* 610; *ELH* 63; *EVaS* disk 8, track 18).

Prayer

Almighty God, our most gracious heavenly Father, as we conclude our study of Esther, may the Holy Spirit whom You have poured out upon us in Baptism bear His sacred witness and seal to our hearts what You have taught us in Your ever-living Word. We praise You that You have hidden Your wisdom from the wise and prudent of this world but have revealed it to babes; through Jesus Christ, Your Son, our Lord, who lives and reigns with You and the Holy Spirit, one God, now and forever. Amen.

Digging Deep
My Personal Study for Week 9

Day 1 • Read Esther 9:20–22

1. What two things did Mordecai do (9:20)?

2. Do you think verse 20 is saying that Mordecai was the human instrument through whom the Holy Spirit gave the inspired words of this book? Why or why not? (Compare 9:32.)

3. The fourteenth and fifteenth days of the month of Adar are appointed for celebration by the Jews. What two specific remembrances are to be made on those days?

a.

b.

4. How were they to celebrate this festival (holiday)?

5. The Augsburg Confession said that "ceremonies and other practices that are profitable for tranquility and good order in the Church (in particular, holy days, festivals, and the like) ought to be observed" (XV 1). Why would this still be so today?

Day 2 • Read Esther 9:23–28

6. The Jews accepted Mordecai's decree to celebrate the festival to commemorate their rescue from the hand of Haman, who sought to "crush and to destroy them" (v. 24).

a. Of what had Haman made use in his plot for destruction (v. 24)? How does this feature of the account play into its irony?

b. How does verse 25 describe the turn of events in relation to Haman?

7. Is this story parallel to any other act of deliverance recounted in Scripture?

8. **Challenge question:** The festival was called Purim, which is a plural form of the word *Pur*. What was the significance of this name? Is there a lesson for us here?

9. How extensive was the obligation to keep the festival of Purim?

Day 3 • Read Esther 9:29–32

10. What was the "second letter" (v. 29)?

11. What additional practices or forms of observance did the second letter add to the festival of Purim?

12. Discuss anything you know about how Jews celebrate Purim today. Do you know what a "Haman hat" is?

13. The festival of Purim was not commanded by God as such. How do we use and misuse the principle of freedom in matters not commanded by God in

a. our individual lives?

b. our church?

Day 4 • Read Esther 10:1–3

14. Does verse 1 itself seem to have any relevance? What purpose does it serve in telling about Mordecai and Esther?

15. What other documentary record of Mordecai's rise to power under Ahasuerus is named in verse 2? The book named has not been discovered. Does this fact disprove that it ever existed?

16. Here at the book's end, was Mordecai being extolled as its true hero? Who is the true hero (or heroine) in the Book of Esther?

17. How do we sometimes forget that men and women are simply servants of God and thus make idols out of them?

Day 5 • Conclusion

18. Looking back on the story of Esther, recall how Haman began and how he ended. What lesson do you see in this, particularly as a believing Christian?

19. Are you disturbed by the fact that the Jews took vengeance on their enemies? Why should we recognize the lawfulness of their actions? How is this to be understood and applied to our lives as Christians?

20. Who is the true "Purim"? In what way?

8. What does verse 17 say happened as a result? What do you suppose lay behind this?

Day 3 • Read Esther 9:1–10

9. Verse 1 records the Jews' gaining of mastery over those who had hoped to master them. It uses the word *reverse.*

a. Give some terms or expressions that are synonymous with this word.

b. Can you think of any other accounts in Scripture where this sort of thing also happened?

10. How did such episodes of deliverance affect the faith of God's people, and how do they still impact Christians today?

11. Verses 2–10 detail the Jews' triumph over their enemies, those who "hated them" (v. 1) and "sought their harm" (v. 2). Which features of this victory are particularly brought out in these verses?

12. What is the one thing the Jews did not do, according to verse 10? Why not?

Day 4 • Read Esther 9:11–15

13. How many were initially killed in the capital of Susa?

14. After reporting this number to Queen Esther, Ahasuerus asked her whether there was anything else she desired. Why do you think he asked this question?

15. What did Esther request? Was this excessive and self-indulgent, or was she genuinely concerned for the welfare of her people? How so?

16. How many more enemies were killed in Susa? Who might these people have been, and how were they made the Jews' enemies? Have you ever experienced anything like this?

Day 5 • Read Esther 9:16–19

17. The Jews in the capital of Susa required two days (the thirteenth and fourteenth of Adar) to dispatch with their enemies, while those "in the king's provinces" needed only one day (the thirteenth). How many of the Jews' enemies were killed by those who lived outside the capital?

18. For the third time, verse 16 reports that the Jews did not do something. (See also 9:10, 15.) What was that?

19. What did the Jews of the provinces do on the fourteenth day that the Jews of the city did on the fifteenth day? Why the different day?

20. Was it sinful to celebrate upon the deaths of so many? Why or why not?

8. Haman was then ordered by Ahasuerus to do these very things for "Mordecai the Jew, who sits at the king's gate" (v. 10). The king added, "Leave out nothing that you have mentioned."

a. What is the significance of the king's referring to Mordecai in the exact words used previously by Haman in 5:13?

b. Read the following passages: Psalm 7:14–16; 9:15–16; 57:6; Proverbs 26:27; and 28:10. What are these verses saying, and on what basis do we know they are true?

Day 3 • Read Esther 6:12–13

9. Describe Haman's state as he returned home after bestowing honors upon Mordecai.

10. Read the following passages: Psalm 101:5; 119:85; 140:5; Proverbs 15:25; and Isaiah 2:11–12. What do these passages say about the proud and arrogant? What is pride, and why is it an "abomination" to God (Proverbs 16:5)?

11. What did Haman's wife say? Why?

12. Apply Isaiah 54:17; Romans 12:19; and 1 Peter 2:23 to our lives. How should we live as we trust God to defend and vindicate us?

Day 4 • Read Esther 6:14–7:6

13. How does verse 14 add to the drama as Haman's plot against Mordecai unravels?

14. At the second feast, Ahasuerus asked Queen Esther to make her true desire known. He promised her up to "half of my kingdom." This figure of speech was used previously (Esther 5:3, 6) and would be used by Herod Antipas in the New Testament (Mark 6:23).

a. At what point in the second meal did the king say these things? Was some devious tactic afoot?

b. Why do you suppose Esther waited until this second banquet to disclose her true petition? How did she model endurance?

15. In your own words, express Esther's request and what she meant by the words of 7:4.

16. What did King Ahasuerus mean by "who has dared to do this" (v. 5)? What precisely was he referring to?

17. Esther identified Haman as the guilty party, calling him a "foe and enemy."

a. Whose foe and enemy does she mean?

b. Why was it ironic that Haman was so described?

c. What word is used to describe Haman's reaction?

Day 5 • Read Esther 7:7–10

18. What role reversals do you notice in verse 7?

19. When the king returned, what did he find Haman doing?

20. **Challenge question:** Summarize how the tables turned against Haman. How is the Christian life opposite this?

21. No sooner had King Ahasuerus exclaimed his outrage than one of the king's eunuch guards covered Haman's face with something probably like the hood used in more modern forms of execution. Standing ready were Haman's own gallows, built for the execution of Mordecai. Ahasuerus ordered Haman to be impaled on it. What was the significance of the eunuch's identifying of Mordecai as him "whose word saved the king" (v. 9)?

22. How can we see in these events the cross and Christ's victory over sin, death, hell, and the devil?

c. Mordecai told Hathach of Haman's plot in which he pledged money to the royal treasury for the

______________________________ of the Jews.

d. Hathach took a copy of the ____________________

____________ to Esther and was told by Mordecai to

command Esther to ______________ with the king

and to ________________________ for his favor.

11. Explain Esther's dilemma in doing what Mordecai wanted.

12. Relate a time when you or someone you know faced a frightening challenge that God placed before you. What help did God's Word give you?

Day 4 • Read Esther 4:12–17

13. What was the point of Mordecai telling Esther the following would happen if she kept silent?

a. She would not escape any more than the other Jews.

b. Relief and deliverance would arise elsewhere.

14. How do Mordecai's words show his faith in God?

15. Mordecai's final appeal (v. 14) to Esther was "who knows whether you have not come to the kingdom for such a time as this?"

a. How did these words move Esther to act?

b. How does the Lord move us to act in service to Him and others?

16. What was Esther's reply in 4:16?

17. Why are the words "Mordecai . . . did everything as Esther had ordered him" ironic?

Day 5 • Read Esther 4:15–5:8

18. Esther was fully aware of the dangers to her life if she appeared in the royal court unbidden. Yet she went. How did she contrast with Vashti in chapter 1, who refused to appear before the king when ordered?

19. What favor did Esther ask of the king? Again, how does this contrast with Vashti? Why did he accede to her request?

20. At the meal, why did the king again ask Esther what she wanted?

21. In 4:16, Esther said, "if I perish, I perish." How do these words express life under the cross? What can we learn from them?

10. Describe Haman's emotions in response to Mordecai's defiance.

11. What did Haman want to do to the Jews? Who was the spiritual force behind this plot, and what was his goal?

Day 4 • Read Esther 3:7–9

12. A practice of divination called "casting Pur" (*Pur* means "lot") took place at Haman's bidding as a means of augury and fortune-telling to make decisions. Here Haman desired to find the most propitious time for his genocidal plot against the Jews. The lot fell on the month of Adar, eleven months in the future. Why did Haman trust in this method? How was he guilty of idolatry?

13. Explain how Haman manipulated King Ahasuerus. Compare this with Satan's temptation of Eve in Genesis 3.

14. **Challenge Question:** In what way does the Gospel of Christ stand against all manipulation? How does this help you in your Christian life?

15. Haman offered to pay ten thousand talents in 3:9. Where might this money have come from?

Day 5 • Read Esther 3:10–15

16. What was the significance of King Ahasuerus giving Haman his signet ring?

17. What was the edict that went throughout the empire in the name of the king?

18. Compare and contrast the response of King Ahasuerus and Haman with that of the people of the city of Susa upon publication of this edict.

19. **Challenge question:** Martin Luther said that the disposition to injure results from the righteousness of the Law. List several of Haman's undesirable traits, and consider how he provides an example of Luther's point.

12. According to 1:19, what kind of woman would be sought to replace Vashti? What does this mean? What application did this have to Esther, and what might it have for you? See Philippians 4:8 and 1 Peter 3:15.

Day 4 • Read Esther 2:1–11

13. Some time later, after Ahasuerus made an unsuccessful attempt to invade Greece, he "remembered Vashti and what she had done and what had been decreed against her." At what conclusion did he arrive?

14. We are introduced to Mordecai in Esther 2:5. How is he identified in verses 5 and 6?

a. Was Mordecai himself taken into captivity in Babylon, or was one of his ancestors taken?

b. If a "Kish" of Benjamin was a distant ancestor of Mordecai, what famous Israelite was Mordecai likely related to? See 1 Samuel 9:1.

15. What relation was Mordecai to Esther? (Her Hebrew name was Hadassah.)

16. An orphan, Esther had no control over her life and was seemingly abandoned to fate. Yet she enjoyed favor from those into whose hands her life was given. For example, how did Hegai treat Esther (2:9)? Why do you think this was?

17. a. How did Esther show a truly submissive spirit? To whom do you think she was ultimately submitting?

b. Discuss the implications for the way we live out our faith, especially in our vocations.

Day 5 • Read Esther 2:12–18

18. The women of the harem were prepared for their presentation to King Ahasuerus.

a. Describe the process of preparation. Why did it take so long? What things do you suppose these women might have taken from the harem (2:13) when appearing before the king? For what purpose?

b. How did the king "interview" the women? See 2:14.

19. Esther's turn came to be summoned to appear before Ahasuerus.

a. What did she do differently from the other women?

b. How do you think Esther won the favor of King Ahasuerus? What can we learn from her?

20. How was Esther like the Christ who "suffered under Pontius Pilate"? How does she also give us a picture of the Church?

b. Read Leviticus 25:23–28 and Deuteronomy 25:5–10. In keeping with these passages, what could Boaz do? Why were men in his position called kinsmen-redeemers? Ultimately, who does Boaz portray for us? See Psalm 107:2; Isaiah 62:12; and Galatians 3:13.

Day 3 • Read Ruth 3

11. Ruth was now well known to Boaz. Naomi undertook to follow up on this fact for Ruth's sake. Read Naomi's suggestions in Ruth 3:1–4. Discuss the meaning of the following phrases from 3:4:

"observe the place where he lies"

"uncover his feet and lie down"

12. Ruth obeyed Naomi (3:6). Boaz awakened and was pleased to find Ruth lying at his feet. What did Ruth ask Boaz? Compare Ruth 2:12. How is the requested action similar to God's act for us in Christ?

13. What was the "first kindness" to which Boaz referred in Ruth 3:10?

14. Ruth spent the night with Boaz (3:14). Yet Boaz praised her as woman of virtue ("worthy woman," 3:11). How do his words allay any notions of improper sexual intimacy that night?

15. What did Boaz do to keep the matter discreet? What was Boaz concerned about? See Matthew 1:19 and 2 Corinthians 8:21.

16. Boaz loaded Ruth's cloak with "six measures of barley" (3:15) and sent her back to Naomi. This amount may have been as much as twice what Ruth previously gleaned in a day (Ruth 2:17). What exceedingly generous gift has Christ given us as a down payment, or pledge, of our final redemption? See Ephesians 1:13–14 and 4:30.

Day 4 • Read Ruth 4:1–10

17. Boaz went to the "gate" of the city. This was a public location where business was transacted and authorities oversaw the civic and judicial affairs of the city.

a. Describe Boaz's manner of dealing with the kinsman (the "redeemer").

b. According to Leviticus 25:23–28, on what basis could this man purchase, or redeem, the property of Elimelech?

18. After initially agreeing to buy the land, the relative was reminded of the law of levirate marriage (Deuteronomy 25:5–6). It may be that over time either custom or the interpretation of the Law came to expect that a kinsman-redeemer would marry the widow of a deceased man even if he was not a brother of the deceased.

a. Why did this closer relative refuse the right of redemption?

b. Did Boaz consider this gain for himself or for Ruth and Naomi? Did he acquire them and their land to possess them or to bless them?

19. How does this act of redemption picture Christ's redemption of us? How does it show a true pattern of love and good works?

Day 5 • Read Ruth 4:11–22

20. Ten elders were gathered to judge this case (4:2). Boaz acted honorably and won the right of redemption, and with it Ruth as his wife. In the blessing of Ruth by the people (4:11–12), with which three earlier women was she connected?

21. What would the birth of Ruth's son have likely meant to her? to Boaz? to Naomi?

22. Who gave the child the name *Obed*? *Note*: this name means "servant."

23. In what ways do our lives spiritually parallel Ruth's?

9. Read Judges 17:6; 18:1; 19:1; and 21:25.

a. All four verses contain a common expression. What is it? What does it have to do with the prevailing conditions at the time?

b. In which texts does the phrase "everyone did what was right in his own eyes" occur? What does it mean?

c. List ways in which this happens in society, in our personal lives, and in the Church.

10. The period of the judges forms the backdrop for the Book of Ruth (Ruth 1:1). How does it help you to understand the setting and the story in Ruth?

Day 4 • Read Ruth 1:1–22

11. According to Deuteronomy 23:3–6, how severely were the Moabites restricted under the Law?

12. Ruth was a Moabitess (Ruth 1:4). Her race, nationality, and religion were different from the people of Israel (1:15). Yet she turned her back on all this and cast her lot with Yahweh (YAH way, the personal name of God in Hebrew), Naomi's God (1:16–17). How did Naomi's life reflect her faith in Yahweh, the true God?

13. Ruth 1:6 says that Naomi returned to Israel because she heard "that the LORD had visited His people and given them food."

a. Read Genesis 50:24 and Exodus 4:31. Discuss what it means for God to "visit" His people.

b. What ultimate act of visitation was also called God visiting His people? See Luke 1:68; 7:16. How did earlier visitations by God relate to this one?

Day 5 • Reading assignments are in each question

14. Naomi attributed the end of the famine in Israel to "the LORD." In our English Bibles, the word *LORD*, with a capital *L* followed by all small capital letters (distinct from *Lord*, where only the first letter is capitalized) represents the Hebrew personal name of God, *Yahweh.* It is not the more generic word *God* but rather the name by which God made Himself known to His people. Often referred to as His covenant name, it distinguishes Him from all other so-called gods. How did Naomi conclude that "the LORD" ended the famine?

15. **Challenge question:** How do the following passages show the strong connection between God's personal name and His grace: Ruth 1:6, 8–9, and 17?

16. Have you noticed that people react differently when you speak of *Jesus* specifically rather than using the generic term *God*?

17. Notice the expression "deal kindly" in Ruth 1:8. The underlying word in Hebrew is *chesedh* (KEH sed). It denotes gracious and kind treatment of others, regarding them as those to whom one has pledged loyal devotion. Why could Naomi invoke "the LORD's" blessing on her non-Israelite daughters-in-law?

b. What honor was given to Mary by Gabriel and by Mary's relative Elizabeth? Did Mary attain this honor?

11. Mere human reason can neither explain nor accept as possible that the child Jesus is truly the Son of God in human flesh.

a. Did Gabriel offer any comment on this apparent impossibility?

b. How did Mary respond to Gabriel's announcement? How should the Christian Church do the same?

12. In Luke 2:19, Mary is said to have "treasured up" what she heard and saw concerning Jesus. What were the things that she treasured, and what benefits did they offer her and the whole world? See Luke 2:10–12, 17.

13. How does Mary show her faith-filled obedience to God's Word in the following passages?

a. Luke 1:35–38

b. John 2:1–5

Day 4 • Reading assignments are in each question

14. What does Hebrews 11:35 specifically say of faithful women in Old Testament times? Read 1 Kings 17:9–24 and 2 Kings 4:8–37 to identify two such women.

15. Read 1 Peter 3:1–6. Peter pointed to Sarah as an example of true devotion to God. She adorned herself with the costly jewels of humility and respect. What motivated Sarah and enabled her in this regard?

16. Read Joshua 2:1–21 and 6:17–25. Two spies ("messengers," Joshua 6:25) secretly entered the city of Jericho prior to an invasion and were received and protected by a local prostitute named Rahab. For this she was promised deliverance for her entire family.

How did Rahab's actions on behalf of the spies dramatically show the connection between faith and deeds?

b. How do we often substitute external busyness "for Jesus" for the true obedience of faith?

Day 5 • Read Luke 8:1–3; 10:38–42; John 12:1–8; Acts 18:1–3, 18–19, 24–26

17. In Luke 8:1–3, we are told that in addition to the Twelve, a group of women disciples followed Jesus.

a. Who were these women?

b. What did they do on Jesus' behalf (Luke 8:3)? Judging by today's business standards, was this a wise investment of their money?

18. In Luke 10:38–42, Jesus was received into the home of Martha and Mary and Lazarus of Bethany. Mary left off her chores to hear Jesus. Martha complained to the Lord, asking that He tell Mary to get back to work.

a. Which of the two women was truly receptive and hospitable to Christ?

19. Later on, Martha's family hosted a dinner for Jesus before Passover (John 12:1–8). While Jesus reclined at the table, Mary anointed Him with an "expensive ointment." She was criticized for being wasteful in doing so. What was Martha doing at this time? How is this situation different than the previous one where Jesus chided her for serving?

20. Read Acts 18:1–3, 18–19, 24–26. Aquila and his wife, Priscilla, were laypeople who assisted St. Paul. After he left them in Ephesus, they helped Apollos fully to understand the Gospel.

a. How did their treatment of Paul show kindness and concern?

b. How do we know that their instruction of Apollos was not an act of public ministry?